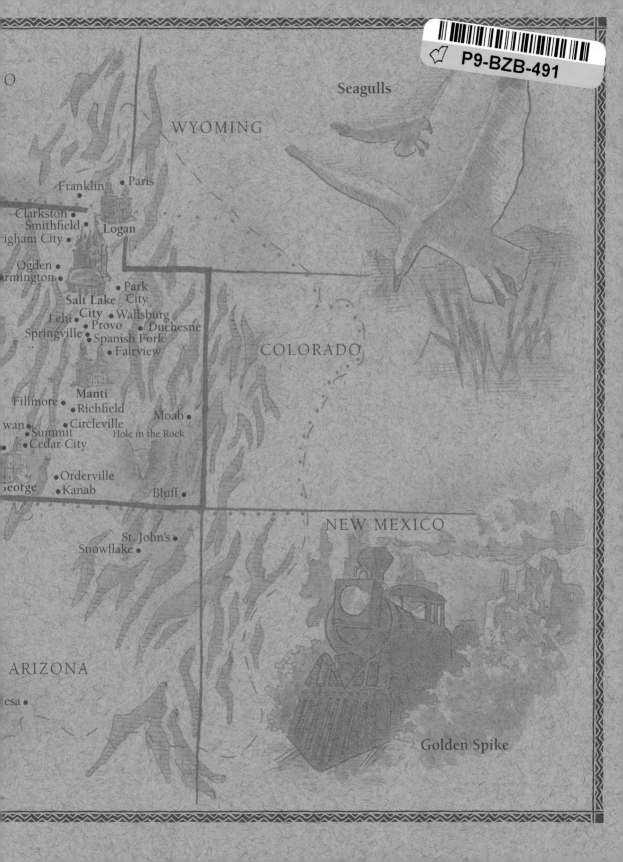

O

Seagulls

WYOMING

Franklin • • Paris

Clarkston •
Smithfield •
igham City •   • Logan

Ogden •
rmington •
             • Park
Salt Lake   City
City • Wallsburg
Lehi •   • Provo   • Duchesne
Springville • • Spanish Fork
          • Fairview

COLORADO

Manti
Fillmore •   • Richfield
wan •   • Circleville   • Moab •
   • Summit   Hole in the Rock
   • Cedar City

     • Orderville
George • • Kanab   • Bluff
                          NEW MEXICO

        St. John's •
Snowflake •

ARIZONA

esa •

                          Golden Spike

———

We had our work, we had our fun and we had our religion. It was a living, burning reality to many of us youngsters that God through Joseph Smith had restored the Gospel of old, had organized His Church according to revelation and had established Zion in the tops of the everlasting hills. We had a conviction that we belonged to a great Cause and that we were needed. With many of my companions I was fired with a determination to carry on the work of redeeming the desert, and of giving to the world the message of the restored Gospel. This determination became the guiding star of my life.

DAVID KING UDALL

GROWING UP IN ZION

True Stories of Young Pioneers
Building the Kingdom

—•••—

Susan Arrington Madsen

—•••—

Published by
Deseret Book Company
Salt Lake City, Utah

Library of Congress Cataloging-in-Publication Data

Growing up in Zion : true stories of young pioneers building the
   Kingdom / [edited] by Susan Arrington Madsen.
         p.   cm.
   Includes bibliographical references and index.
   Summary: Includes longer reminiscences which describe experiences
of Mormon youth growing up in Utah between 1847 and 1900, shorter
excerpts which complement these writings, and letters written by
children.
   ISBN 1-57345-189-4
   1. Pioneer children—Utah—Biography—Juvenile literature.
2. Mormon children—Utah—Biography—Juvenile literature. 3. Mormon
youth—Utah—Biography—Juvenile literature. 4. Utah—Social life
and customs—Sources—Juvenile literature. 5. Frontier and pioneer
life—Utah—Sources—Juvenile literature. [1. Mormons. 2. Utah—
Social life and customs. 3. Frontier and pioneer life—Utah.
4. Children's writings.] I. Madsen, Susan Arrington.
F826.G76   1996
979.2'0083—dc20
                                                          96-22032
                                                             CIP
                                                             AC

Printed in the United States of America   18961
10   9   8   7   6   5   4   3   2

For Emily, Rebecca, Sarah, and Rachel,
who live the legacy

CONTENTS

Preface

This volume is devoted to the experiences, sacrifices, and contributions of nineteenth-century Latter-day Saint children and adolescents, and shows the significant role they played in helping to establish Zion in the mountains and deserts of the West. What better time than the 150th anniversary of the arrival of the first Mormon children in the Valley to recognize that young persons laughed, cried, spun, cooked, milked, planted, harvested, and prayed alongside their parents in this new land.

I have chosen to let children who grew up in the Great Basin tell their own stories. Who can describe the dark, damp experience of sleeping in a dugout more effectively than the child who shivered each night in such a primitive home? Who better to tell of eating porcupine for dinner, or chewing on an old hawk boiled all night in a pot, than the boy who was hungry enough to swallow such a grisly meal? These boys and girls were there, and their own words have a power greater than any third-person retelling could convey.

This book contains three kinds of excerpts. First, there are longer reminiscences that describe the youthful experiences of the writers. Second, there are many shorter excerpts that enrich and complement the longer narratives. The shorter entries appear as sidebars; each tells a single incident or makes an observation that adds detail and color to our understanding of pioneer living.

The third category is a rare and remarkable collection of "letters to the editor" written by children and published in the *Juvenile Instructor* beginning in 1897. The *Juvenile Instructor* was a Church periodical, the masthead of which proclaimed it to have been "designed expressly for the education and elevation of the young." These early letters add the innocent and spontaneous voices of children. The other stories are mostly told by adults looking back on and describing their own youth.

As with most books, limits had to be set for this project or it could never have been completed. I have left out far more than I have included, but the excerpts here are representative of the more than 200 life histories I have studied.

Limits had to be placed on age, place, and time. This book focuses on the experiences of youth under the age of twenty, growing up within the bounds of what was then called the State of Deseret and later the Utah Territory, between the year 1847, when the first Mormon pioneer company entered the Salt Lake Valley, and the turn of the century.

For those desiring to read more about the earlier or later lives of these young pioneers, the titles and locations of the longer histories are provided at the end of each chapter. The list of sources at the end of the book directs the reader to the sources of the shorter excerpts.

To illustrate this book, we have included more than a hundred photographs of young people from the Great Basin area in the nineteenth and early twentieth centuries. Many of these children are unidentifiable, but their photographs give us a feel for the period of time in which they lived, the clothes they wore, and the friends and pets they cherished. Sources of these photographs are listed at the end of the book.

To make the book more readable, spelling, grammar, and punctuation have been modernized in some instances. Other than this, words have not been changed except when necessary to clarify the meaning of a sentence. Sentences and phrases have sometimes been deleted, especially in longer entries, in places not critical to the narrative. The future married names of young women are included in parentheses in the chapter headings.

Many people contributed to the creation of this book. I express thanks to the LDS Church Sesquicentennial Committee for suggesting that Deseret Book Company publish the volume. I am deeply grateful to the staff of the library and archives of the Historical Department of The Church of Jesus Christ of Latter-day Saints in Salt Lake City, especially Richard Turley, Managing Director; William W. Slaughter, photograph archivist; and Melvin Bashore, reference librarian and indexer extraordinaire. I appreciate the friendly assistance of Ann Buttars and her associates at the Utah State University Merrill Library, Special Collections and Archives. Staff members in the Special Collections and Manuscripts Department of the Harold B. Lee Library at Brigham Young University and the Utah State Historical Society were generous with their help.

Those who gave excellent research suggestions and provided me with interesting histories include my father, Leonard J. Arrington; Lyndia Carter, Oregon-California Trails Association; Ross Peterson, Director, Mountain West Center for Regional Studies, Utah State University; George and Maria Ellsworth, Reed Durham, Sue Arnett, Roy Davis, Glenn Damron, Michael Johnson, Marie A. Done, Steve Bower, Lon Bower, Lorna P. Belnap, Gaylen and Elaine Ashcroft, Deleta Holland Selvage, Amy Howells White, Janet Seegmiller, Marjorie Conder, Mary Jane Fritzen, V. Philip Rasmussen, and the late A. J. Simmonds.

I appreciate the refining editing suggestions of Willis L. Pitkin, Jr., of the English Department at Utah State University, as well as the guidance of James C. Jacobs, professor of children's literature at Brigham Young University.

My husband and friend, Dean, spent long hours reading the manuscript and making valuable suggestions. Together we have laughed and wept over what we have read.

I greatly appreciate the opportunity Deseret Book Company has given me to become acquainted with these sturdy, young Latter-day Saints. They are pioneers in the truest sense of the word.

Susan Arrington Madsen
July 2, 1996
Hyde Park, Utah

Introduction

n April 1847, Brigham Young's advance pioneer company left Winter Quarters, Nebraska, and crossed the Great Plains to the Great Salt Lake Valley. The original company included a hundred and forty-three men, three women, a variety of horses, mules, oxen, cows, dogs, chickens . . . and two children.

Lorenzo Sobieskie Young and Isaac Perry Decker, both of whom were six years old, would forever have the distinction of being among the first white children to arrive in the Valley and become permanent residents of Utah Territory.

Both these boys would live to an old age and contribute in their own ways to the settling of this new territory. Lorenzo, or "Sibbey," spent his life as a sheepherder in Utah and Idaho. The son of Lorenzo Dow and Persis Goodall Young, he married Sarah Black and was the father of twelve children. In 1922, when the Church held the "Diamond Jubilee of the Coming of the Utah

Pioneers," Lorenzo attended (at the age of eighty-one) as the only living member of the original pioneer company of 1847.

Isaac, the son of Isaac Perry and Harriet Page Wheeler Decker, carried United States mail by Pony Express and was acquainted with such well-known frontiersmen as Kit Carson and Jim Bridger. He is said to have been able to "ride the meanest horse and rope the wildest cow." Isaac married Elizabeth Ogden; one of their eleven children, Charles Franklin Decker, later became the mayor of Provo, Utah.

Among the several teenagers who were also part of that first company was fourteen-year-old Andrew Purley Shumway. Andrew burst into tears when his father, Charles, announced his plans to leave his son with relatives while he went west with the advance company. After a consultation with Brigham Young, permission was granted for young Andrew to come with his father. Andrew had been baptized in 1842 in the Nauvoo Temple baptismal font and was healed by Brigham Young of Rocky Mountain spotted fever during the westward trek. Andrew would later be called to serve as the first bishop in Mendon, Cache County, Utah. He would also serve a mission to Great Britain, and would eventually settle with his family in Franklin County, Idaho.

Children have played a part in every chapter of the history of The Church of Jesus Christ of Latter-day Saints. From fourteen-year-old Joseph Smith, whose First Vision in 1820 in Palmyra, New York, heralded the restoration of the gospel of Jesus Christ, to eight-year-old Alice Minerva Richards, who saw angels at the dedication of the Salt Lake Temple in 1893, the youth of the Church have shared in the sacred experiences that come with being part of the Lord's work. But children have seldom been the focus of our written history.

Official histories of the Latter-day Saints have understandably emphasized the activities of the prophets and their associates in organizing the Church and supervising the work of the kingdom. In recent years more recognition has been given to the tremendous contributions women have made in settling the West and furthering the work of the Church.

Children have remained, however, largely silent partners in the drama of our past. Recent studies show that in 1847, nearly half of the 1,611 Latter-day Saint settlers living in the Salt Lake Valley were under the age of nineteen.

The histories of these young people help us understand the countless hours they spent doing the essential work of settling the West. We learn of the food they ate, the clothes they made and wore, the homes they built and lived in, the games they played, and the schoolteachers they loved, feared, and would never forget. We begin to understand what it meant to be a child in settlements that were also in their infancy. We read of experiences with Native Americans, many of whom became the settlers' close friends. We learn of courtships, of accidents, and of death, and we feel a child's sense of loss at the passing of a parent, brother, or sister.

The panorama of youth is as broad and colorful as life itself. In its own way, youth is as profound as any other part of human experience, and children are as central to any epic adventure as the parents and leaders who nurtured them. These families came west because of their testimonies of the restored gospel of Jesus Christ. Their absolute commitment to the cause of Zion kept them from giving up and returning to their former, more comfortable, homes and livelihoods. Nearly half of those who endured hunger, disease, harsh weather, and other formidable obstacles were children and teenagers. A noble price was paid by people *of all ages* to establish a safe haven in the West where Zion could grow and the work of the Lord could be nourished. When the voices of Zion's children are heard, our history is more complete and some of its most interesting actors and actresses have their turn at center stage.

PART ONE

The Arrival

s immigrating Mormons emerged from the Wasatch Mountains through Emigration Canyon, they saw before them the Great Salt Lake Valley. Sunburned, ragged, and footsore, they were grateful to reach their promised homeland.

Reactions to the valley, however, were mixed. Some considered it the most beautiful sight they had ever seen and spontaneously shouted for joy as they threw hats and bonnets into the air. Others saw a wasteland, dry and treeless—a haven only for lizards, crickets, and rattlesnakes.

But even those who were at first disappointed with their place of refuge were grateful to be far from the angry mobs that had persecuted them so hatefully in Ohio, Missouri, and Illinois. To those who had experienced such persecutions, the valley's peace, safety, and religious freedom were far more important than the beautiful homes and farmland they had left behind.

Many children buried one or both of their parents along the Mormon Trail. The arrival of these young people in the valley was more than just the end of the journey. It raised a whole new set of questions: Who will take us in? Where will we find food to eat? Will we have a roof over our heads when we go to sleep tonight?

Thankfully, most settlers who had arrived earlier in the Valley had big hearts. Usually by nightfall, tears were dried and heavy hearts were lifted as some good soul pulled up to Pioneer Square and invited a lonely child or two to climb into his wagon and join his family. Personal histories are filled with stories of orphans, and even whole families, being welcomed into the homes of generous Latter-day Saints who were willing to stretch their already sparse resources a little further.

Thus many began their new lives in this place which God prepared, far away in the West.

Christopher Alston

Born: September 8, 1853, Southport, Lancashire, England
Parents: James and Ann Molyneaux Alston

Christopher traveled to the Salt Lake Valley in 1864 with his eight-year-old brother aboard the ship General McClellan. *The two boys crossed the plains that year in Captain Joseph S. Rawlins's company. Their mother stayed in England, coming to the Valley the next year. Their father was deceased.*

In the above photograph, Christopher is seated on the far left.

We arrived in Salt Lake City September 20, 1864. I was then eleven years old, having celebrated my birthday twelve days before arriving here. I must relate the welcome I received on the first day and night in the Salt Lake Valley. In the morning, about 11 o'clock, we came out of the mouth of Parley's Canyon, where we were met by a number of men and teams. The first words of greeting I heard were, "Come here, my boy, and hold your cap." I came near the wagon from which this voice came. There was a man kneeling in the bottom of the wagon on some

I drove the oxen to take mother and the children down near the river to gather cattails for filling bed ticks and pillow cases. There is not much said about cattails these days but many a pioneer would have suffered dreadfully from cold during those terrible winters, if it had not been for those comforting, comfortable cattails, which made such warm, soft beds.

—*Margaret Simmons*
(Bennett) (Beck)

straw, and the wagon was nearly filled with peaches. He scooped up his double hands full of peaches and put them into my cap, then scooped up another handful and put them into my cap also, and it was full of lovely peaches, the first I had ever tasted in my life. "There," he said, "now eat those." He kept handing out peaches until his load was given away. I ran to our wagon where my brother lay very sick and gave him some peaches, then divided the remainder with the teamster and my custodian, John Ollerton, who had brought me from England, then I ate the rest. Now imagine, if you can, an eleven-year-old boy who had walked 1,100 miles and had an 1,100 mile appetite, and had never tasted a peach before in his life, having half a dozen nice peaches to eat!

We traveled down the Sugarhouse street for four miles. There we were met by my uncle—my mother's brother—who took us home to his place where they were threshing, and where a thresher's dinner had just been served. We washed and sat to a table—the first time since leaving England—and ate a most glorious dinner not sitting on the ground and eating out of a camp skillet with a butcher knife.

In the evening my cousins, Walter and James Wilson, took me up to a big molasses mill run by a big water wheel, where molasses was being made. The furnace fire under the boiler lighted the yard. Lanterns were placed here and there so the men could work during the night. Girls and boys had numerous small fires, where they were making molasses canes from the skimmings which the men tending the boiler had given to them, and all of the "kids" wanted to give the immigrant boy some of their candy. Then my cousin peeled a stalk of sugar cane for me to eat, and he said, "Christopher, you stay right here, we are going across the road, we will be back soon." They crossed the road, climbed a fence and ran down into the field and came back with big ripe watermelons, and they had not planted those melons. I was given a big section of a luscious melon to eat, and I thought "This is Zion" most truly and I was in ecstacy. My mother and [her] three youngest children came to Utah the following year, having similar experiences, trials and hardships.

As the oldest of five children, Christopher shouldered much of the responsibility of providing for his mother, brothers, and sisters, because his father was deceased. As a boy, he would take a yoke of oxen up into the canyons and bring down logs to sell for firewood. He worked at Promontory Point to help complete the railroad at age fifteen. He married Annie Charlotte Chapman Smith (an adopted daughter of Elder Orson Pratt) in 1874. They became the parents of eight children, including twin sons. After her death in 1917, he married Marie Olsen. He worked as a carpenter, building bridges, homes, hotels, factories, and meetinghouses. He also helped build the Salt Lake Temple. Christopher was a member of the Salt Lake police force and was the justice of the peace in the Sugar House precinct. He loved missionary service and temple work. He died August 25, 1930, in Salt Lake City, Utah.

We finally got to the mouth of what they call Emigration Canyon, where we could see Salt Lake City. We all thought it was the most pleasant sight that our eyes had ever beheld.

The Captain took the lead down from the mouth of the Canyon and we followed him. All that had any place to go to left. But me and eight others that had no relations or friends to go to stayed by the wagons, built our camp fire, cooked and ate our supper and were sitting around the fire when a gentleman came up to us.

Shaking hands with all of us, he asked if we had any relatives in the country, and how we had fared while crossing the plains, and where we came from. We answered his questions and then he asked us if we had anything to eat. We told him yes. "Well," he said, "I want you boys to stay right here and make yourselves as comfortable as you possibly can until you each get a place to go to."

We thanked him very kindly and promised to do as he requested, and then he told us who he was, and that his name was Brigham Young. We were camped in President Young's yard.

—*William Henry Hill*

....
SOURCE:
Autobiography. *Our Pioneer Heritage* 8(1965):35–38.

Samuel Roskelley

Born: January 1, 1837, Devonport, Devonshire, England
Parents: Thomas and Ann Kitt Roskelley

Samuel immigrated to Utah in 1853 at age sixteen.

n crossing the bench from the mouth of Emigration Canyon to the Bluff east of the city, our eyes were feasted with the sublime sight we had desired so long to see and as we caught a view of [Salt Lake] City, the throbbing of our hearts increased and our anticipations were realized—the promise of the Elders at Devonport [England] fulfilled—"I had come to Zion." . . . The . . . Salt Lake Valley looked lovely beyond description.

The people of [my company] seemingly all had friends to go to but me. I did not seem to have any. I seemed to be a stranger in a strange land. Perhaps my outward appearance was so repulsive that no one felt disposed to offer me a home or place to stay 'til I could find employment. I certainly was a sad looking sight—for I owned no clothing but an extra shirt except what I stood upright in that I had worn nearly all the time since I left England. It was so filled with dust and dirt, had been torn, patched and mended, was [sewed] and re-sewed while upon my body that I could not get it off my person, so it was about skin tight and I dare not stoop and had to sit down very carefully for fear of exposing my nakedness. All this came about [because of] my clothing having been stolen at Laramie [Wyoming]. Notwithstanding I thanked the Lord for His kindness and mercies to me in giving me the privilege of coming to Zion. I felt my lot a hard one as I knew no one to unburden my feelings to or ask advice from, but I knew God was my friend and I laid my case before Him and feeling that He would open up my way for good. . . .

Bro. Nelson Spafford of Springville drove up with a team and wagon and inquired for a young man that came in with the last company of emigrants and had no home. I heard him and spoke to him. He scanned me from head to foot thinking, no doubt, I was a hard-looking subject. He said he had been recommended by some friend of his to find me as he was called on a mission to Fort Supply and wanted someone to stay with his family through the winter. He lived some 60 miles south and if I wanted to go with him and stay the winter he would give me a home and plenty to eat if I would do his work and look after his family. I thought it would be the best step I could take and told him I would do the best I could for him. . . . I got into the wagon and started for Springville without further ceremony, arriving there on the evening of the next day. Seeing my pit[i]able condition for clothing he gave me some of his partially worn clothing, as at

With the exception of a doghouse, I have lived in all kinds of houses from mud on. Our new home was just one large room. Father made the foundation of rock and mud, about 18" thick. This was left to dry thoroughly, then another layer would be added and dried, then another layer, and so on, working each day, until it was raised to about an 8' square. Then all of our belongings were moved in before the roof was placed. The roof consisted of two poles placed across the center and at first the wagon cover was stretched over cornerwise until the branches of a few trees and reeds and leaves and such as could be procured could be placed thereon. This foliage was made into bundles and fastened together in rows over the logs, and the children had to tromp this down. Then a covering of mud was placed over all. When a heavy rain came, of course the mud would leak and allow the water to come thru and every one had to manage a brass kettle or other utensil.

—*James Bryant*

When we arrived in Salt Lake Mother was so worn out with sorrow and with sitting in the wagon holding the sick children that she was so bent over, she could not straighten up. People said she looked like she was sixty years old. We landed in Salt Lake City on September 30, 1866. We had been one hundred twenty-nine days since we left Hamburg, Germany, and we had left our home about ten days before that. There had been four children when we left, now I was the only child left.

—*Caroline Pedersen (Hansen)*

that time clothing of any kind was very scarce and high priced. I was strange to every kind of work done in this country and whatever I went at I made hard work of it and it took me all my time to get the wood, milk the cows and do the chores for Sister Spafford and her child. Bro. Spafford soon left for his field of missionary labor and I thought I had [the] immense labor on my hands of caring for his wife and child. I had to work an ox team on shares to get the wood, but the winter passed very pleasantly. . . .

When Spring came Bro. Spafford came home and could do his own work so I was no longer needed by him. I felt impressed to go to Salt Lake City.

I got an opportunity to ride with one of the Brethren and went directly to President Young's and saw him and asked for work, [I] told him who I was, where I came from and what I had been doing since my arrival in Utah etc. He seemed favorably impressed and gave me work at $5.00 a month with board lodging with Bro. Hamilton G. Park. The first article I drew for pay was a pair of buckskin pants, that meant nearly three months wages. In dry weather they would come about half way between my ankles and knees and in wet weather, would flippity flop on the sidewalk every step I took. . . .

I think about the 4th of June 1854 was the first time I ever saw Pres. Young. At the time I applied for work. I was deeply impressed with the man—a prophet of God! A Seer and Revelator. I looked upon him almost with awe, he was the man of all men I desired to become acquainted with—and I supposed that was the reason I was so bold in going to ask him for work for my unusual [timidness] would have led me in any other direction. . . .

[*Samuel, age eighteen, was employed by President Brigham Young to help with the Young family's needs and projects.*]

My wages were increased to $15.00 a month and board. . . . President [Young] was finishing the Lion House and he set me to cleaning up and preparing the rooms for occupancy. I helped his families to move into their new quarters about the last of November 1855. The President boarded half of his time in the Lion House and when not there it [fell to] me to call the family together and pray with them and to ask blessings at the table, etc. etc. This used to be a hard task for me [shy] as I was and many times I should have shrunk from it had it not been [my] duty.

[President Young] went to Fillmore as governor of the territory to attend the Legislation, before leaving he met me and told me to continue living in the Lion House and take care of

My most vivid remembrance was of the time Brother Brigham Young came to visit us. How excited we all were. . . . The Sunday School children were lined up on each side of the road in front of the school house, each dressed in his best and holding banners and flags. Our Sunday School teacher told us when he passed our class we were to bow, some of us thinking he was looking directly at us bowed several times for fear we would forget. How we loved him. When he talked we listened for every word. He was so kind, so earnest in all he said, we were certain he was a Prophet of the Lord and we loved him with all our hearts. He was a wonderful leader and I have always thought there was no other man on the earth who could have led our people across the dreary plains with such wisdom and order and love, unless he was chosen of the Lord.

—*Katherine Perkes (Harris)*

In Brigham City we lived in a [one-room] dugout near a creek. Mother kept our dugout clean and dry. She was very much a lady, very refined, and she always made the best she could of what little she had to do with. She used to think I was a harum-scarum child and too full of fun and laughter. She often told me to smile instead of laughing aloud.

To make our dugout more homelike, Mother would wash sand from the creek bottom and scatter the clean white sand over the clay floor. Then we picked wild currant leaves from the bushes on the banks of the creek and spread these over the floor and we had a pretty green carpet.

Because our single room was so very small, it was necessary for me to sleep on a pile of straw on the floor under [Mother and Father's] bed. My pile of straw was covered with a sheet and I had quilts over me.

The entrance to our dugout was down some stone steps and the dirt was piled high on each side of the steps. One day I remember a big blue snake came down over this bank of dirt, poked its old head in at the door and waved its head around. I was not afraid of it; we were only afraid of the rattlesnakes that stayed up on the hills among the rocks.

—*Alma Elizabeth Mineer (Felt)*

his families, as I was the only man he was leaving around his premises, except the clerks in the office. I thanked him for the confidence he reposed in me and told him I would do the best I could. . . . It took me all my time to do what was required of me.

After the President had been gone a few weeks the measles broke out among the [Young] children and we had a serious time. Nine were down at one time. . . . For five weeks I never took my clothes off except to change my underclothing and all the sleep I would be able to get was when so much exhausted I could go no longer, administering so much day and night took all the vitality out of me. Often when I would take my hands off the sick child I would rest with exhaustion. I fasted much to benefit the sick and pled with God to restore them to health. Clara Decker Young's [son] Jeddie was very sick and I exercised myself over him very much but after a lingering illness of several weeks his spirit left its body to go to a better place on 11 January 1856. I believe I mourned over it as much as I ever did over one of my own for I loved the child dearly. I am sure sister Clara felt I was devoted to her child's interests and remembered me with gratitude. It [was] a gloomy winter.

. . . While conversing with sister Clara after the death of her darling, the question of having faith in God was spoken of—she said, "It has been a severe trial of my faith to lose my child in the absence of its father—my husband—but it has taught me a lesson to rely upon the Lord more and my husband less. For I do not know but I have thought too much of my Brigham." I write this as a lesson to my own dear family—not to expose Sister Clara's private feelings as expressed to me in all confidence.

During the Spring and Summer the famine for breadstuff was very severe—as the grasshoppers had cleaned the fields two previous years to an alarming extent and [the price of] flour had run up to fabulous figures—entirely out of the reach of the poor. [President Young] had succeeded in buying a few loads of flour from Bro. Reese and stored it away. He . . . reduced all dependent upon him to half pound of flour per day. Out of that, much would be given away daily to the poor, who would call and the family would divide and many times the box would be scraped for some poor mother who represented that her children were hungry and perhaps half an hour afterward it would be scraped again for some other poor soul under similar circumstances. The flour box always yielded a little every time it was scraped for the poor. Thus have I seen the goodness of God and the faith of Brigham Young and his family manifested in helping the poor. . . . Many of the Saints in Utah suffered for want of bread during those hard times, while many

I remember when I was quite small we children would get sagebrush and fill the corner and in the evening would put a little on the fire at a time to make light enough so Father could read the Book of Mormon to us. We liked so well to hear him read. Mother would be sewing or knitting. I have seen my father get up with the Book of Mormon in his hand and say, "How I wish I could make my voice sound to the ends of the earth and teach them the glad tidings of the gospel!" He read the Book of Mormon through seven times and was reading it again when he died.

—*Sabra Jane Beckstead*
(Hatch)

If we ever found anything [that did not belong to us] we were taught to take it to the Tithing Office, where the owner could call for it. That rule was observed all through the settlement for many years, and was a very fine custom, as it taught the children to be honest, and not to appropriate things to their own use that did not belong to them.

—*Mary Elizabeth Woolley (Chamberlain)*

resorted to pig weeds, thistle roots, mustard leaves and every kind of vegetable mixing with bran . . . for food but no one died of starvation that I am aware of.

In August, 1856, one evening after the workmen had all gone home, I stood looking into the street from the porch over the Lion of the Lion House, when suddenly I felt someone's arm around my shoulders and neck. Turning my face I discovered it to be Pres. Young. Said he—calling me by name, "I think you had better go on a mission." As soon as I could recover from my surprise I answered—"I don't know what you want to send me on a mission for. I don't know anything." He answered—"I'll risk you in that matter."

Samuel Roskelley served two missions in England. He married six wives and had thirty children. He was superintendent of Cache County schools, a captain of the Cache County Militia, and a major in the Smithfield Battalion. He was also mayor of Smithfield and president of the Smithfield Cooperative Mercantile Association. A bishop in Smithfield for eighteen years, Samuel also was recorder for the Logan Temple for nearly twenty-eight years. He died February 10, 1914, in Smithfield, Cache County, Utah.

SOURCE:
Journal. Holograph. Utah State University Special Collections.

Mary Field (Garner)

Born: February 1, 1836, Stanley Hill, Herefordshire, England
Parents: William and Mary Harding Field

Mary is shown holding a baby in the photograph above.

he journey west was a long and tiresome one, filled with many trials and hardships. Some died on the way and were buried by the roadside, fire being burned on their graves so the Indians would not disturb their final resting place. . . . We were put on strict rations, but during all these hardships no one complained. The Saints rejoiced for their knowledge of the Gospel of Jesus Christ, and their spirits were undaunted by suffering. Westward, ho! Westward, was the cry of every Latter-day Saint. Just to be in Salt Lake Valley with our Prophet and leaders and the rest of the Saints was the greatest desire of our hearts.

As we came down through and out of Emigration Canyon, the beautiful valley of the Great Salt Lake stretched out before us. We all stopped our wagons and came together to look and wonder and thrill at what our eyes beheld. At last, we could see our journey's end. We drove on down into the city—a little over a year old—dotted with log and adobe cabins and tents. We were soon passing a large bowery, under which church services were being conducted. It was mid-afternoon. Our old friend, Dr. Meeks, was at the meeting and was sitting near the outside. When he heard our wagons come rolling by, he looked and saw Father on lead, so he ran out and stopped us. He got up onto the seat with Father and took us to his place—and we all thanked the Lord for that—and for our safe arrival at our destination, after such a long, hard journey.

Of course, the first thing was to get poor, tired Mother down and into the log cabin; and the next thing was to unyoke our tired, hungry oxen and get them and our cows and horses to water and pasture. Mrs. Meeks was already home cooking dinner as if she was expecting us; but she did have to put more into the pots. We had green corn for dinner, and I thought I had never tasted anything so good in my life.

—*Anna Clark (Hale)*

We held campfire meetings, sang songs, and tried to enjoy ourselves the best we could under the existing conditions.

We arrived in Emigration Canyon late at night. We hurried to make camp, had a little to eat and went to bed hungry and cold. When we woke up the next morning, everything was white with snow. It was not a heavy snow, but it made everything in the valley cold and wet. This was our first morning in Utah. The Saints in the Valley had been informed of our condition and where we were camped, so they came to cheer us up and to bring us a hot breakfast. Oh! What a good hot breakfast it was, and how thankful we were to get it! We were all so hungry. They had prepared good hot potatoes and gravy, some meat and hot bread. I had never tasted such a good potato. We did not have any potatoes. After we ate breakfast we all felt warm and much stronger to pack up again, break camp, and start on, knowing our journey was nearing the end. I shall never forget the first sight of the Great Salt Lake Valley, and the rejoicing in every heart, to be able to be with the Saints of God and to again find a haven of rest from mob violence. We were received with kindness by the Saints and made welcome to Zion, the valley of peace and happiness.

By the time we arrived in the valley, the Saints here numbered several thousand. After remaining in Salt Lake a short time, we came on north and settled in Slaterville, Utah, where we took up some land and then built a log house and here we engaged in farming. The land had never been plowed, so we had to grub the sage brush, which was a very slow process. Then it

had to be plowed with the oxen. It was a struggle with the soil for a few years to make it produce enough crops to live on, but we were happy and content to have a home of our own to live in. This was the first home we had ever owned in America, and we could now look forward to peace and prosperity again.

The crops of 1854 and 1855 had both failed because of drought and grasshoppers, but the grasshoppers did not eat mother's crops. We had been taught by both Prophet Joseph and Brigham to divide with each other, so we divided our grain and vegetables with the Saints. The saving [of] our crops we attributed to the over-ruling power of God. Some of the cattle died through exposure to cold weather and lack of food, yet we were happy, we no longer had to fear attack from the heartless mob.

Our one home was three log rooms in a row. We lived in the first one, had our tools in the middle one and our cattle in the rear room.
  —William Andrews

The roof was made from limbs, brush and mud, and it was not an unusual sight to see the roofs of these mud houses covered with sunflowers and stink weeds.
  —Jane Sprunt (Warner) (Garner)

When I was eight years old they told all the children over eight to be baptized in Sanpete Creek, so Father said I could go. When I got out of the water my sister was there and helped me dress. The bishop told us to come to the church at night, so I went all alone to be confirmed. None of my family knew where I was. After I was confirmed I was so tired I went to sleep on the front bench. My family hunted all over town for me. They were afraid I might have been taken by an Indian. At last they came to the church just as the man was putting out the last candle and they found me peacefully sleeping on the bench.

—Alma Elizabeth Mineer (Felt)

Now by this time I was a grown up young lady and still had my red, curly hair, which . . . had its attractions for the Indians. [One] day an Indian chief came to our door, and to our great surprise it was the same Indian chief whom we had [met while crossing] the plains. He made us understand he had followed us here and . . . wanted me to be his bride. Of course, mother refused him again, but he would not go away. He sat beside our door for three days. This was an old Indian custom before demanding his bride. After the three days were over, again he asked me to be his white bride. He offered mother many, many ponies, beads and blankets for me and said he would make me queen of his tribe, that I could have a tent of my own and his other squaws could be my servants, and he would make me happy. Mother refused and told him to go away. Still he was not satisfied. He asked me to go with him back to his tribe. I refused and [t]old him I would never go with him, that I was white and must live with the white people, and to please go back to his Indian tribe and not to bother me again. With lowered head and bent shoulders, he went away sorrowing. I have never seen him since.

Mary Field married William Garner Jr. November 1, 1856, in Slaterville, Utah. They became the parents of ten children. They farmed in Slaterville and Hooper. As a pioneer mother, Mary herded cattle, carded and spun wool, sewed dresses and overalls by hand, and gathered sagebrush for fuel. *She supported her husband while he served a mission to England from 1882 to 1884. He died in 1915, leaving her a widow for twenty-eight years. When Mary died July 20, 1943, at the age of 107, she was the last living person to have seen the Prophet Joseph Smith. She lived ninety-nine years after his martyrdom. Her autobiography includes a stirring testimony of his prophetic calling.*

SOURCE:
"The Last Leaf," Autobiography. Photocopy of transcript. LDS Church Archives.

We reached Salt Lake City the 5th of October [1860]. Mother and I stood there on Emigration Square and had no friends to meet us. A brother came and asked us if we had no place to go. We said no. He said, "You shall not stay here. You shall come with me." With thankful hearts we went with him to his home, in company with some other emigrants. All he had was one room and shanty, but he had a big heart.

The next day was Conference, 6th of October, and mother and I went. To me the people looked like angels, in contrast to us, all sunburnt and black. I said, "They are too pretty to come in contact with." The singing was heavenly. The meeting was in the Bowery on the Tabernacle Square and I saw President Brigham Young, the Prophet of the Lord. I could not understand all he said but I had learned some English in my childhood at home and that helped me now. Mother and I got along the best we could, by the help of the Lord, till my brother with his family arrived in 1862.

—*Johanne Marie Thomassen (Berg)*

PART TWO

The Early Years

oung people living in the Utah Territory in the late 1840s and early 1850s lived in primitive, frontier conditions. After their arrival in the valley, whole families often lived in wagon boxes, sometimes for days or even months. Such a family's next home would be a dugout in the side of a hill, a breezy log cabin, or a house built of sun-dried adobe bricks. Roofs were made of timbers and branches covered with dirt or sod. When it rained, there were never enough buckets or bowls to catch the muddy water as it dripped through the roof. Lucky was the boy or girl who had an umbrella to huddle under inside a leaky home during a downpour.

Pioneer children and their parents worried about not having enough food. Frost in late spring and early fall destroyed many of their fruits and vegetables. Wandering cattle and horses sometimes ate or trampled gardens. Some years, just when a bountiful harvest seemed assured, hordes of ugly, black, oversized crickets would come in from the desert and devour their crops.

There were other worries, too. Nearly all children who lived in the Utah area before the turn of the century encountered Indians. Though most of the settlers' experiences with Native Americans were positive, cultural differences sometimes created unfortunate misunderstandings and fears. Indian men and women saw nothing wrong with walking unannounced into a white settler's cabin or dugout. They were attracted by freshly baked bread, pies, and biscuits. They considered food to belong to everyone and so they helped themselves, causing nervous children to hide under beds, or, if their parents were not home, to run to neighbors for protection.

Nevertheless, friendships developed between Indians and Mormons, young and old. Many times they played together, worked together, fished, hunted, wrestled, rode horses, and taught each other new skills. They helped each other when difficulties arose and mourned for one another's tragedies, sufferings, and disappointments. All in all, there was enough patience, generosity, and understanding between Saints and Indians to maintain a remarkably good relationship.

Although conditions were primitive in those early years, hard work and good humor ultimately prevailed. The Latter-day Saints had made a covenant with God to give their all to the building of Zion, and they fulfilled that commitment.

John Fell Squires

Born: April 5, 1846, Putney, Surrey, England
Parents: John Paternoster and Catherine Harriett Fell Squires

 e finally arrived at our destination [the Salt Lake Valley]. This was on the thirtieth day of September, 1853. . . . The first winter we occupied a little shack about 12 x 14 near Union Square. We lived in the back and Dad barbered in the front part. The [partition] between our living room and the shop was a pair of old blankets strung on a string so that we could hear everything said or done. If we wished to size up the bunch all we had to do was to go to a peek hole which were quite numerous in those blankets. . . .

Up to this time I began to get Americanized and was up to all kinds of mischief. . . . I held my own with the boys in the neighborhood when it came to throwing rocks, dust or mud, hair pulling and tearing clothes. I have known my Mother to burst into tears many a time after recognizing me and

investigating what clothes were left on my anatomy after a free for all with the children of Zion [who, their] parents would say, had to [bear up] the Kingdom and bring about its final success.

Our new home in the 20th Ward consisted of two rooms unplastered, [with] unplaned floors. This house was built in the sage brush like others in that vicinity. The houses were few and scattered, all without fences, making it convenient for borrowing purposes, which had become a common habit.

During the coldest nights, it was necessary to take what little food we had to bed with us in order to keep it from freezing. On more than one occasion when failing to do this we had to eat our breakfast with an ax on the table. The small ditch which supplied us with water would be frozen up for weeks at a time making it necessary to melt snow for all purposes. I have carried water many times from the Eagle Gate a distance of eight blocks.

During these times a circumstance happened to our home that I think is worth mentioning because it will show how united the people were and how willing to help a neighbor when in trouble. One morning just as we were getting up one of those east winds blew the flimsy roof off

One evening about sundown I was walking up after water and we had to go about a third of a mile to get it. When I came back I was carrying two bucketsful and not looking ahead and I walked right into an Indian who had his arms out. I was so frightened for a minute that I spilled both of the buckets of water. The Indian laughed and picked up the buckets and went up to the well and refilled them and carried them up to the house for me.

—*Comfort Elizabeth Godfrey (Flinders)*

our [house] and landing most of it [across] the street, breaking the rafters, sheeting and raising the devil generally. Father said, "This is lamentable, as I have no money to buy lumber or nails to replace the roof."

Mother cried, my sister cried, my little brother Walter was already crying through fright, and . . . I joined in the chorus so that we made some noise which attracted the neighbors. They soon gathered around to take a look and to sympathize with us. As they were leaving they would say, "Squires, we will be back to give you some help after breakfast."

I will say right here that we had a much better and stronger roof on our house before sundown than the one that blew off, besides [kindling] wood to last a generation. Why, half the town was there. Some brought boards, others rafters, ceiling [joists], shingles, nails, hammers, saws, everything that would cut a [board] or drive a nail. Talk about flies on sugar, why our lot was the liveliest spot in town that day and by the time the last nail was driven I concluded it to be the noisiest day I had ever spent. . . .

We passed through the grasshopper siege of three or four years duration and by the time they were done and ready to leave for good, we were a sorry looking bunch. I will give you a little idea in regard to the way they treated us.

The advance guard [of grasshoppers] began to arrive one morning, and by night they had all landed without a single accident. The kind of breed that paid us this visit could fly as far and as high as they wished. The sky was so dense with them one could scarcely see the sun, and it was all a fellow could do to face them when they

In 1868 my brothers were called to settle in Bear Lake Territory, and Grandmother and I accompanied them. No sooner had the crops started to grow, when millions of grasshoppers descended upon our farms and in spite of all the work we did in trying to rid ourselves of them, they destroyed nearly all of our crops. When the grasshopper hordes finally left, they flew out into the Bear Lake and were drowned and the fish ate them in such quantities that many of the fish also died. The wind blew so many of [the grasshoppers] upon the lake shore that they were stacked two or three feet deep.

The next summer it was the crickets that destroyed practically all of it; so we were . . . forced to go through another winter of cold and hardships with but very little flour. If it had not been for the fish in Bear Lake, it is doubtful if we could have survived.

—*Eliza Ann Lamborn (Murphy)*

One time while we still lived at White's Fort my mother kept missing the cream from her pans of milk which were set in the cellar to cool. At first she thought the boys were skimming it off to put in their "bread and milk," but they all declared that they knew nothing about it. One morning one of the boys went into the cellar a little earlier than usual and he saw a large striped snake skimming the cream off the milk as skillfully as a person could do with a skimmer. It is needless to say what happened to the "cream-fed" snake. From then on the milk was left undisturbed.

—*Sarah Ann Murdock*
(Lindsay)

began to light. I will say right here that I have never seen the same species since. They had a business activity which was marvelous to behold as they never closed their [chops], or jaws until every thing of a green nature was devoured right down to window blinds and green paint. A green [sprout] stood no more [chance] outdoors than I would in the ring with Jack Dempsey [the boxer]. If a male or female appeared outdoors dressed in green they would be driven to cover or uncover in less than no time. . . . If they could eat all the bark from a shade tree, which they did, it would not take them long to eat up a fellow's pantaloons when the color suited them. It was a [mystery] where they came from or went to after filling their mission. All that we knew was that they left the whole surrounding country brown and leafless and ourselves looking blue. Just [think,] one thousand miles from [a] market, too late in the season to plant another crop, little or no food in the country, so that famine stared us in the face. People who have not passed through these conditions can hardly understand the hardship and feelings of those who have.

I have been without bread weeks at a time, just living on roots, segoes, weeds or anything chewable, always hungry and never satisfied. I have seen my Mother cry many a time when trying to portion out what

little she had to her children. My little brother who could not understand the situation would say, "I'm hungry and want some bread." Mother's answer was, "I have not a bit in the house for you. . . ." [Then he would ask:] "Why don't you get some then?" And she could not explain to his understanding why. After my brother Harry had said his prayers at Father's knee and was bidding him goodnight, he never failed to say, "Father, can I have all the bread I can eat after harvest? Why don't they have harvest now?". . .

[John's father was called to serve in Echo Canyon during the Utah War of 1857, and was absent from the family for several months. During his absence, the Squires family temporarily moved south to avoid Johnston's Army. After John's father returned, they moved back to Salt Lake City.]

Dad opened up a [barber] shop and made money pretty fast. . . . I hung around the shop most of the time to gather up dirty towels, sweep

We used to have to go to a little house that was built in the center of Spring City [to be baptized]. This house had water flowing into it and they had a tin sort of tub . . . and it was slick on the bottom. That water was ice cold. This day [in November] that I was to be baptized my mother thought it was such a cold day that she put a winter dress on me. It had bands of velvet on it for trimming. When I got down in the water and it got soaked up with water, I had to be hauled out of there.

—Vera Blain (Larsen)
(Downard) (Sorensen)

One Sunday I dressed up in my brand-new red dress and red pantalets and went proudly down to show them to Aunt Betsy and Uncle Fawn. Aunt Betsy had a flock of white geese and when they saw me in my bright red dress they stretched their long necks and screamed and hissed towards me. They knocked me down and pecked me and stomped and flapped me with their wings. I screamed with all my might and Aunt Betsy ran with a broom and beat the geese away. Poor me, I came in glory, but all my splendor was gone. It was a sad looking child that Aunt Betsy had to wash and cuddle back into smiles again. When the tears were all wiped away and I was eating a piece of luscious cherry pie I felt better but I never wore my red dress again.

—*Sarah Ann Murdock (Lindsay)*

out the hair, and kill lice. Everybody was lousy and happy. The bull whackers bred them by the bushel in crossing the plains and saved them to dump onto the Mormons. . . .

After the first rush [of barbering] was over and Dad could dispense with my valuable assistance, he hired me out to a lawyer at one dollar per week, which shows how valuable my time really was. I was employed as an unskilled laborer, general roustabout, swept the office, blacked his boots, fed the dog, washed the ice and stuck it into a bucket, and stole his . . . peaches, . . . making myself handy and useful to him. As time moved on, Dad hired me out for the winter to Geo[rge] W. Thatcher. He was then living at the old Chase Mill where the city park is now situated. My work consisted of cleaning stables, horses, buggies and harnesses, so that I soon began to smell like the whole combination. Many a time I was visiting Mother with Thatcher's pet race horse when he thought me to be sleeping in my little bed. Dad would let me go to school when he could not find anything else for me to do. This is why I am so bright.

Mother died . . . about this time and while I lost considerable interest about home, I had no desire to run away. . . . It was then that I concluded to learn the barber trade and I stayed with that nasty, stinking, skin scraping, fidgety profession.

John Fell Squires married Alice Penn Maiben, whom he had first known when they were crossing the plains at the ages of seven and six, respectively. He observed her courage during the trek and later wrote, "She was gritty and tougher than myself."

They were married August 7, 1868, in Salt Lake City and became the parents of twelve children, three of whom died in infancy. John and three of his sons served full-time missions for the Church. He cut stone, held important positions in the U.S. Forest Service, and worked as a barber, sometimes attending Brigham Young. He died February 10, 1933, in Logan, Utah.

SOURCE:
Autobiography. Photocopy of transcript. LDS Church Archives. Also *Ancestral Histories and Pedigrees of Joseph W. Poppleton and Flora Christena Squires,* written and compiled by Anna Rae Allen Poppleton, 1992. Utah State University Special Collections.

I well remember George A. Smith, John Taylor and Brigham Young. The latter gave me a word of praise and a nickel. I remember seeing Apostle George A. Smith crossing our yard when a gust of wind blew off his wig.
—*Edward Hunter Snow*

Annie Taylor (Dee)

Born: November 4, 1852, Lostock Gralem, Cheshire, England
Parents: John and Ann Sanders Taylor

n the winter of 1860, there was a great deal of snow and it was very cold. I was a little girl only eight years old, and of course, was unable to go to church often. One day I sighed and said, "Oh, dear, I must go to meeting or Brigham Young will cut me off the church." The family laughed, but I thought that Brigham Young had nothing to do but to keep track of every little girl in the church, and know whether she came to meeting or not. . . .

In the spring, father rented a small store on Main Street [in Salt Lake City] and started in his business [as a] merchant tailor. . . . There were two other men, shoemakers by trade, who rented the back part of the store from father. . . . They made shoes for us children out of the tops of father's boots. He had worn out the bottoms on the plains. . . .

Once my sister and I got some pieces of [material] the folks brought with them, and each made herself a doll's quilt, all nicely padded with cotton wool. Some time after, father was making a coat for a man. He had been trying to get some [padding] for the coat but could not find any in town; so he asked my sister and I if we would give him our little quilts to pad the

EVENING DEVOTIONS

coat. This we gladly did; and I have often wondered what the people who had the coat thought, when it wore out, to find two doll quilts on the inside. We all had to do the best we could, and it was necessary at times to make odd make-shifts, as all clothing and material was brought to Utah by freight in wagons drawn by mules or oxen.

In 1862, Connor's army entered Salt Lake City. The streets were lined with people gathered to see the soldiers. I was one of the onlookers. The troops marched with the band first, then the soldiers with the officers on horseback. There was also a train of wagons drawn by mules. The troops looked dusty and tired as they marched along State Street and went to the place that is now called Fort Douglas. . . . It helped my father's business in a short time as he had lots of work in making uniforms for the officers.

One day I was in father's store with my younger brother, John, when an officer from the Fort came to get some work that father had done for him. When he paid for it, father did not have the change, so the officer asked me to go and get

Mother was very strict in the observance of the Sabbath and attended the services in the Tabernacle every Sunday, taking me with her. She taught me to pray from my earliest remembrance, and when one of the general authorities of the Church arose to speak, she would tell me his name and inform me that he was one of the men I prayed for every night. In this way I became acquainted with the presidency of the Church and the Twelve Apostles at a very early age, and was so impressed with them through my mother's teachings that all through my life I have had a reverence for the general authorities of the church.

—*John M. Baxter*

The Bear Lake district was the summer home for many of the Ute, Sioux, and Shoshone Indian tribes. When summer came, you would see a long train of them traveling in single file come over the mountain and into the valley where we lived. When they all arrived the flat lands next to the lake would be covered with several hundred tepees and wigwams.

The Indians would not swim in the [Bear] Lake because they feared monsters. They said they had seen them and that their bodies had the shape of a large log.

One day while Grandmother and I were at the corral, an Indian chief and his son came riding up the road. When they saw us, they leaped from their horses and the chief ran, shouting and with blankets flying, to Grandmother. He threw his arms around her and cried, "Grandmother Bailey! Grandmother Bailey!" I screamed in fright, but the chief quieted me and told me that his name was Tabby and that he liked Grandmother very much for they had been old friends at Spanish Fork. Although it had been several years since he had seen us, he still remembered Grandmother's goodness to him. We asked them to stay to dinner, which consisted of bread and molasses. This they did and they visited with us two or three hours before continuing on their journey.

—Eliza Ann Lamborn (Murphy)

the change for him. When I came back he gave me a dime which pleased me very much as that was the first money I had seen for some time. My brother wanted me to get just a little candy, but I thought of grandmother, and how she disliked to be in the dark at night, so I got two tallow candles with my dime. My brother, of course, was disappointed, but grandmother was pleased, so I felt better about it, but was sorry I could not do both. . . .

When I was about fourteen, my sister and I joined the Tabernacle Choir. Services were then held in the old Tabernacle, where the Assembly Hall now stands [on Temple Square]. We were still members of the choir when the new Tabernacle was first used, and we sang at the funeral of President Heber C. Kimball. I think I have never seen such a storm in June in my life as there was on the day of President Kimball's funeral. There was terrific thunder and lightning, and the rain just poured down. As rubber [galoshes] were not very common at that time and we had to walk, there we sat throughout the service with our feet sopping wet. . . .

When we girls went to choir practice at night we went through the east gate [of Temple Square]. The Temple had been started and there was lots of work going on. We would walk along the foundation of the Temple, which was sixteen feet wide, so it was easy to walk on. The square was like a workshop. There was not much machinery at that time, but the stone blocks were fastened by chains to the breach pole of a wagon and drawn from the quarry to the Temple Block. . . .

The people of Utah were always very fond of music and it was introduced into plays whenever possible. . . . When choruses were introduced in the plays at the Salt Lake Theater, members of the Tabernacle Choir were called upon to sing them, and as my sister and I both were members of the choir, . . . we were chosen to sing in a number of plays. In a performance of Macbeth there were about fifty members of the choir, men and women, to sing the witches' choruses. . . .

On one occasion Madam Scheller played Cinderella [at the Theater]. Fourteen girls took part in this play [including] . . . my sister and myself. . . . We practiced quite a while. We all had to start at once, and with the same foot or all was wrong. I remember how Brother Sloan, our teacher, was tried. Our dresses were longer than they are now, and he would say, "Now Miss So-and-So, don't think that I can't see your feet! You started with the wrong foot. Start again." So we would go to the back of the stage all in a line with crossed hands and start over again; but we finally got it. When the play was at last produced it ran fourteen nights and a matinee. . . .

The theater and dances, which we enjoyed very much, formed most of our amusement. When we went to rehearsals at the theater, the girls were

Our home was built near a slough. One spring we had a long rainy spell, mother awakened one night by a tapping and bumping of pans. She awakened father but having no light he stepped from the bed into water up to his knees. Mother called to us children to see if we were safe and then father put out his hand to see if the baby, sleeping in a borrowed cradle, was all right. The cradle was not there. Panic stricken, he felt around in the darkness and finally located it where it had floated to the other side of the room, giving Will, like Moses, a ride in a cradle.

When morning came father carried us one by one on his back, out of the house. A spring of water had seeped through the spongy ground and gushed up through our fireplace. Brother Hunter had an unused dug-out which he kindly let us live in until the water could be bailed out of our home and fires built here and there on the floor to dry it out.

—Jane Sprunt (Warner) (Garner)

When I was eight years of age . . . we stayed several days at the Lion House, in Salt Lake as guests of Aunt Zina [wife of Brigham Young] who was a dear friend of Grandma's. I distinctly remember one circumstance, when we had assembled one evening, in the large family prayer room, President Young called me up to him, admired my long yellow hair, took me on his knee & kissed me, saying I was certainly his girl because he claimed all those with sandy hair.

—Ida Hunt (Udall)

never allowed to go home alone at night. President Young's double carriage was always at the stage door to take to their homes all the girls who did not have escorts. Fred Holland, the coachman, used to be impatient if we did not hurry, but we didn't mind him. All the girls going the same way would go in one load, then he would leave those at their homes and return for more, and so on, until all were safely home. That is an example of the thoughtfulness of President Young. He was very careful of young girls to protect them from every harm.

Annie Taylor married Thomas Duncomb Dee, an immigrant from Wales, on April 10, 1871, in the Endowment House in Salt Lake City. They lived in Ogden and became the parents of eight children. Annie's husband became a business partner of David Eccles. Together, they founded the Utah Construction Company, the Ogden Savings Bank, and the Amalgamated Sugar Company, as well as many other businesses. In 1910, after the premature deaths of her husband and oldest son, Reese, Annie and her children funded the construction of the Thomas D. Dee Memorial Hospital in Ogden. Annie encouraged and paid for many women to have their babies in hospitals, thus minimizing health risks associated with at-home births. Annie served her community as an active member of the Civic League, the Martha Society, and the Child Culture Club, and she was the governor's appointee on the Utah State Council of Defense during World War I. She served as president of the Ogden LDS Eighth Ward Relief Society from 1909 to 1923. Annie died April 11, 1934, in Ogden, Utah.

SOURCE:
Annie Taylor Dee, *Memories of a Pioneer,* 1930. LDS Church Historical Library.

Lorenzo Southwell Clark

Born: May 14, 1852, Chesterton, Cambridge, England
Parents: Benjamin Thomas and Ann Southwell Clark

My parents, with their family, arrived in Salt Lake City in the autumn of 1853. . . . Our home was built in 1854, a one-and-one-half-story adobe structure. It contained a large living room and was by far the biggest house in the neighborhood; many people besides our own direct family found shelter beneath its roof, and I remember neighborhood gatherings being held there.

The evenings at home with father reading to us from the Bible and other books which came into his hands, stand out in my pleasant memories. At such times, mother sewed, the other half-brothers and sisters did something useful with their hands, and we little ones, sometimes for a special treat, shelled and ate carefully hoarded squash seeds.

My earliest impression is one of work; the idea and ambition of everyone

I remember the dreadful grasshopper plague of 1897. The sun was darkened by them and there were no screens on windows or doors so they came indoors. They were of great torment to infants and larger children. They would get in the folds of lace curtains and eat holes in them. They also ate holes in the starched articles hanging on the clothes lines and spit "tobacco juice" on other articles. Everything in the gardens was eaten until there was not a green blade in sight. Two acres of corn that was owned by our next door neighbor was eaten down to the stalks. Chickens fattened and thrived on their grasshopper diet. Since that year people have stored plenty of wheat and have never ceased talking of famine.

—*Sarah S. Moulding (Gledhill)*

around me seemed to be to accomplish more and do it better than anyone else. Work was more conspicuous than play, even among the young children who were expected to carry wood and water, run errands, feed the chickens and pigs, kill crickets and grasshoppers on sight with sticks, gather lucerne seed, and help as far as possible with the gardening. Immediate playmates were scarce in our scattered farming district, so we learned our ways mostly from each other. . . .

The real spirit of the pioneer group was industry and everyone scorned the idler. . . . In bad grasshopper and cricket years we were close to starvation; our rations then . . . were two small pieces of corn bread twice a day. We were fortunate if we could add milk.

The time came when we had good crops; then the family, both married and unmarried members, would gather together often in our home and feast upon such bounties as the Lord saw fit to give us. Then we would sing songs and hymns, tell stories, enjoy each other's presence, and always speak of the blessings of the Lord. Such occasions were really joyous. . . .

Dancing was a favorite community entertainment, but I never tried to dance for want of opportunity. At an early age I learned to play the "fiddle," so while I attended every local dance, my duty and portion was to sit at one end of the room on a chair placed on top of the table, and make the music while I watched the girl I adored dancing with the other fellows.

In 1858 we were part of "The Move." I was six years old and remember a little about our stay in Spanish Fork. Our dugout was about 14 or possibly 16 feet square, and nearly four feet deep. . . . [For a roof] weeds were placed over willows and dirt on top of them. We descended [to the entrance] by means of about six steps on a slant, like stairs. There was a doorway, but if there was a door to close, I have forgotten it. We took no chickens with us, but our neighbor, whose name was Flint, had quite a flock. One day a small speckled hen wandered over to see us, descended our steps, strolled through the open doorway, and chose to lay an egg on my mother's bed. We took it over to Brother Flint's and explained what had happened. To my surprise he sent it back again in a most friendly manner.

I used to watch the snakes crawl in and out among the willows in our ceiling and was in no way afraid of them. Once father killed two of them with a hatchet. . . .

While we were there [in Spanish Fork] we planted corn. . . . We did not remain long enough to harvest it. On the return journey [to Salt Lake City], I drove the yoke of cattle we brought across the plains, old Tom and Charley. They didn't need much driving but seemed to know the way. I remember the smiles and tears when we drew near to our own "home, sweet home."

It was while in Spanish Fork that summer that I learned one of the most impressive lessons of my life. My father had married a widow with five children, who came with the Martin

Father and two of my older brothers went to a little town called Coolidge in New Mexico and they got a job cutting timber for the Southern Pacific Railroad. He left Mother and the rest of us at home. We didn't have food then and often we children went to bed crying from hunger.

One night an Indian came and knocked at our door. He was carrying with him a half of a mutton. Mother was frightened at first and then she broke down and cried and asked the Indian why he brought this to us and the Indian said, "Papoose, heap hungry."

—*Roy George*

One day as we were walking to the Warm Spring we were on 2nd West street just East of where the West Side High School is now located. The powder magazine or arsenal as it was called, located where the State Capitol is now located, blew up. We heard the explosion, Lew shouted "get behind trees"; all the others did, but I watched the spectacle.

One large rock, about the size of a large wash tub, came hurtling through the air. I watched its flight as I have many times watched shooting stars. This rock landed about 30 feet from where I was standing. Every [pane] of glass in the windows of Salt Lake City was broken.

There were only 5 or 6 fatalities. . . . A lot of boys were playing baseball in a slight depression just west of the Arsenal. All were knocked down, none were hurt. The rocks were thrown over them and landed much farther away.

—*William Shipley Burton*

Handcart Company. This group, added to those he already had from the two previous marriages, made a large mixed family. Rations were short, as only a limited amount of provisions could be carried so far, and these had to last till our return to Salt Lake. The result was that I was hungry most of the time. I realized that I was the eldest child of my parents, and that the one who controlled the rations was my very own mother. So I waited till she and I were alone, when I went to her and told her I was hungry and asked if I might have an extra piece of bread and butter. She held my face in her hands, looking down at me lovingly with tears streaming from her blue eyes, and explained that she must not give more bread to me or there would not be enough for the children of the two other mothers. I was such a child that I thought I, not she, should be the one to cry as I didn't get the bread; but in time I came to know the meaning of it all and to bless my precious mother for that lesson.

Crickets continued to bother us more or less for a number of years in various sections of the country. I remember them definitely in 1859, and also the Heaven-sent seagulls devouring them. [The crickets] would travel in flocks, all moving in the same direction. Sometimes we could walk a mile or so without seeing one, [then] we would come to a place where they would almost cover the ground from sight. One peculiar characteristic of the flocks of gulls was that in the middle of the day they would all rest upon the ground for an hour or two, then all go to work again.

My next impressive memory after the "move" is of becoming a herd boy, which was the regular employment of the pioneer lad of our locality as soon as he was old enough, and which kept him busy from early spring to late autumn. . . . We found [ways to] play and also learned many things. Sometimes we neglected our cows, I am sure. One accomplishment of the boys who were small enough, was to brace themselves against the tires of the wagon wheels, holding tightly to the spokes, hands on one rim and feet opposite and so go for a ride. Because the oxen moved so slowly it wasn't really as dangerous as it sounds, but we thought it was a thrilling experience. . . .

There [were] some pleasant experiences for us herd boys. We learned to swim, run and climb, and even wrestle. We became acquainted with the native vegetation and the wild life. We were expert at digging sego [roots to eat]. Sometimes we bothered the birds' nests. . . . We knew the holes, nests, eggs, and habits of such common wildlife as rabbits, night hawks, snakes, gophers, lizards and horned toads, as well as the birds. . . .

[At the age of sixteen, Lorenzo went to work for the railroad company in Echo Canyon. During this time, he had the following experience:]

We had a few days before the engineers were ready for us and we spent them in playing ball, wrestling and mountain climbing. We boys located an eagle's nest in a cave near the top of a cliff, and attempted to investigate. There was some scrub oak growing on the very top of the ledge. I removed my shoes and two strong boys each took hold of one of my feet with one hand,

The Indians used to pass our home a lot as it was on the main highway to Montana. They often camped right near our place and had their wigwams there, and when they had gone my sister and I used to go and pick up beads they had left behind.

Mother and Father were good to the Indians and used to give them flour and supplies. One time some Indians were going by our place and they had a sick papoose and they left it with my mother as she was a doctor and they thought she could make it better. She kept it about a year but it died and is buried in our lot in the City Cemetery.

—*Annie Hermine Cardon (Shaw)*

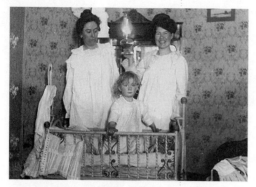

The first I knew of the gulls, I heard their sharp cry. Upon looking up, I beheld what appeared like a vast flock of pigeons coming from the northwest. . . . Their coming was like a great cloud; and when they passed between us and the sun, a shadow covered the field. I could see the gulls settling for more than a mile around us. They were very tame, coming within four or five rods of us.

At first we thought that they also were after the wheat, and this thought added to our terror; but we soon discovered that they devoured only the crickets. Needless to say, we . . . gave our gentle visitors the possession of the field. As I remember it, the gulls came every morning for about three weeks, when their mission was apparently ended, and they ceased coming.

Do I love the seagulls? I never hear their sharp, shrill cry but my heart leaps with joy and gladness, for I know they saved my father's family and his people from fearful death.

—*John R. Young*

and held tightly to an oak with the other, thus letting me down head first over the edge of the cliff. The parent birds were in the air sometimes high up, then darting straight down as though they would strike me with their beaks, claws, or bodies, but turning sharply aside with a screech and shooting straight upwards again ready for a repeat. I saw the nest with two fine well-grown eaglets.

The boys pulled me up, and when I described the young birds they thought they must see them. So we found a long, nearly straight branch from a service berry bush and, making a lasso of my buckskin shoestrings, tied it to the end of the stick and over the cliff I went again as before. This time I brought back one of the eaglets, then went over again and brought up the other one. They were about the size of a full grown hen and rooster, with a thin covering of pin-feathers, and of a very light brown or dirty white color. They let us examine them and appeared to be wholly unafraid, making no effort to get loose. They made entertaining camp pets until they were able to fly away.

Our clothing was simple and plain, with many patches because of tearing it on willows and bushes. Our feet were bare, and became so thickened and hardened on the soles that we could walk anywhere, and climb over rocks and rough places without inconvenience. We took a lunch in what we called the "dinner sack." Indians were plentiful and whenever they could, they would take it from us. If we saw them coming we would try to eat it up before we were overtaken, even though it might be early morning. Three of us played a little joke on these Indians one day. We ate the contents of our bags, then filled them with squaw berries. We met our enemies and they gave us chase; we held our own for about half a mile, when they caught me. There were six or seven of them with bows and arrows, so I could do nothing but submit. They took my dinner sack and with great gleeful chattering thrust in their hands. When they pulled out the squaw berries, they looked at me in a way that showed their great disappointment, then made some unpleasant demonstrations with their bows and arrows; after which I was permitted to meander back to my cows.

I seem to remember almost every detail of this [time] and count it as one of the outstanding periods of my colorful youth.

Lorenzo married Mary Rachel Wagstaff on August 17, 1874, in Salt Lake City, Utah. They became the parents of seven children, five of whom lived to adulthood. After his seventh child was born, Lorenzo served a mission to the Southern States. A talented musician, he was a member of the Tabernacle Choir and played the piano, organ, and fiddle. Lorenzo created a "grandchild pasture" on a quarter acre of property, where his grandchildren spent many happy hours playing. He died December 19, 1923, in Salt Lake City, Utah.

SOURCE:
Autobiography. *Heart Throbs of the West* 9(1948):391–96.

When Brother Brigham Young and his apostles and party arrived, the streets of our little village [Mt. Pleasant, Utah] were lined with children to welcome them. Everyone loved Brigham Young and as they came along in their wagons we all waved our handkerchiefs. Brigham Young was in a carriage with black curtains. We were all dressed up in our best to greet our leader. . . .

After the banquet they held a meeting in the meetinghouse, which I attended still dressed in my new calico gown and straw hat. Before dismissing us, Brother Brigham said, "All you brethren who have teams, put the covers on your wagons and take your families and follow us from place to place around this valley, and I promise you in the name of Israel's God, he will water your crops." It had been a very dry summer and our crops had suffered for want of water, but when we left the meetinghouse the rain came down in torrents and my new dress and hat were drenched. I knew then, when only a child, that he was a prophet of God, and I have never forgotten that testimony.

—*Alma Elizabeth Mineer
(Felt)*

Barbara Gowans (Bowen)

Born: February 13, 1855, Liverpool, Lancashire, England
Parents: Hugh Sidley and Betsy Gowans Gowans*

*Barbara's mother's maiden name was also Gowans.

e crossed the plains in Milo Andrus' company. Father drove a team of oxen; Grandfather and Mother walked all the way, and Grandmother rode in the wagon to take care of me and two other children who were not old enough to walk. We arrived in Salt Lake hungry and weary, thankful we were at our journey's end, having traveled by ox team and foot over one thousand miles. Grandmother, in telling later of her experience, always expressed thanks for the bed of straw in the tithing yard, where she rested at her journey's end.

Our family remained in Salt Lake a few days and were then sent out to the Government Reservation in Rush Valley. We lived in the barracks which were built into the sidehill by soldiers. The winter was a hard one with not much to eat. The flour was so black with smut that we could hardly eat the bread. Father and Alex Frazier, a young man who had come with him from Scotland, one day ran down a rabbit, as they had no gun with them, and furnished the food for our first Thanksgiving dinner in Utah. . . .

Grandmother and I used to go along the ditch where the willows grew to gather nettles to eat. She would tell me to grip them hard, then they would not sting. I can remember sitting down to eat nothing but greens. We used nettles, pigweed, and redroot. Also, we dug and ate the sego lily roots which were considered a delicacy. Later Grandfather had the finest garden in town, and when I was old enough to tell vegetables from weeds, he kept me busy weeding during the summer. My brother Robert, age seven years, and I would go with Grandfather to the field to clean out the weeds in the corn and potatoes. While walking to the field I would break the milkweeds and by the time we came back the milk would be dry. We used it for gum. We also gathered balsam from the pine trees in the canyons, boiled and strained it, and this made our best gum.

Grandfather paid for the lots by the skill of his hands. He made rush-bottom chairs and baskets, bringing the rushes from Rush Valley which grew in abundance around Stockton Lake. He showed me how to shape a little basket of rushes over my hand, just a little one from the short lengths of rushes that were not used for the chair seats. I used these for bird nests.

The first school I went to was located on Main Street; William B. Adams was the teacher. School was held three and four months during the winter. The next school was located on north

The Indians were in [our] neighborhood. We needed water, mother picked up the water bucket and said that she would go to the Loveless ditch nearby to get some water. She told me not to be afraid, that she would be back before they could get to our place. She left the door open. The Indians saw her going to the ditch, so they ran to our place. Mother had just taken some biscuits out of the oven for dinner. I saw the Indians coming, so I took the biscuits and crawled under the bed. The bed had a valance so I thought I was well hidden; but the squaw came in, looked under the bed, spied me and the biscuits and asked for a biscuit. I was so frightened that I gave her all of them. Mother was angry when she returned; she had used the last bit of flour we possessed for those biscuits.
—*Lillie Barney (Murnane)*

I was well acquainted with Black Hawk and his squaw. My father and mother were in the choir and they used to have choir practice at our place. Black Hawk and his wife used to come and listen to them sing and were very interested. Mrs. Black Hawk was very pretty.
—*Lovenia Nicholson Sylvester (Berry)*

[One day] I went down to take the men in the fields some homemade root beer. Our farm then was down on the river bottoms and some men were rounding up some cattle. Grandfather Ringrose and I were seated on a wagon tongue and the cattle sort of stampeded and headed right for us. We were sure scared and grandfather hollered for me to "slap up the umbrella." I did and that is all that saved us, [the umbrella] scaring the cattle away from us.
—*Annie Elizabeth Frost (Clarke)*

First West. A Mr. Bowering was [the] teacher. I took my lunch while attending this school. Lunch consisted of bread and bacon grease, which I enjoyed. The games we played were Run Sheep Run, Pump Pull Away, Dare Base, and Hop Scotch. We played keeping house in a room built in the mud wall on each side of the south gate. . . .

Father asked me one morning to herd the oxen up on the hills. Another girl was herding calves. We got so busy hunting flowers and giving them names that I forgot all about the oxen. When I thought of them they were gone. I could not find them, and Father walked three days carrying the yoke before he located them. It was my first and last time as a pioneer herd girl.

My grandfather made me and my two brothers each a chair and a table to eat from or play with. He also made me a pair of stilts. They were nicer stilts than any of the other children had. Grandfather also made us kites, and he made me crochet hooks out of the coarse combs after the teeth were all gone. Grandmother taught me [how] to knit and Mother taught me to sew and crochet. . . .

In 1867, when the crickets were bad, men, women and children would go out and drive them into trenches, or piles of straw and willows, and burn them. I would go with Father and Grandfather and help in this battle for existence.

When I was sixteen, Emily Warburton and I went to Salt Lake City to learn telegraphy. We rented a room from a Mrs. Ure in the Fifteenth

Ward. We batched and our parents sent in provisions. We were in Salt Lake three months being taught in President Young's office, and we saw him every day. We celebrated Pioneer Day in Salt Lake City in 1871 and participated in the telegraph float in the parade.

In the fall of 1871 the Western Union opened an office in Tooele and Emily and I were the operators. I will never forget the first message I sent. Emily did not want to send it. I was very nervous. I tried, but all that was received was the address and the signature. The gentleman who sent the telegram, thinking perhaps that we might have been nervous, went to the Western Union Telegraph Office in Salt Lake City to inquire about the message. It was shown him and had only the address and signature. He sent the message from there. He was very kind about our mistake and never made any trouble for us because of this grievous error. . . .

In 1872 Father was called on a mission to England. After he had been gone several months, Emily left the [telegraph] office and I held the position alone until Father's return. I also assisted in the post office and express office, both of which were in the same building with the telegraph.

In 1874 the Young Women's Retrenchment Association was organized in Tooele. I was chosen one of the counselors. There were not any lessons printed at that time, consequently the officers of the young men and the officers of the young women met together to formulate a plan that would be satisfactory in carrying on the winter's study. Different plans were discussed and it was finally decided to form some resolutions. I

We owned a dairy. One night [Aunt Nora] woke up hearing a noise in the cheese room about one hundred feet away. She thought by some mistake the trough that ran the cold water in and through the vat to cool the milk overnight in a double-boiler affair had been turned out of the double boiler. It sounded like it was running on the wooden floor. She put on her slippers and walked down there in her night clothes. It was about one hundred feet. She put out her hand to open the door into the cheese room when she found herself right in the arms of a black bear who was trying to gnaw his way through that wooden wall into the cheese room. He could smell the cheese. Aunt Nora whirled and went one way around the cheese room and the bear went the other way and [they] met face to face the second time. Aunt Nora said . . . it has never been determined who was the more scared, her or the bear.
—*Torrey L. Austin*

When [the grasshoppers and crickets] could fly they kept them in the air with sheets, caps, and other things so that they could not rest to eat the green grain. Rollers [which ran by flutter-wheel water power] were placed across the canals. The rollers . . . ground them up, especially the crickets that grew in size 2 x 1 inch. These were driven into canals and smashed by two rollers, one above the other. Another way was to place straw in piles around a farm, when straw was available. [The crickets] would gather by the millions on [the straw] in the evening to keep off the cool ground and then we would burn them. By these simple means and great diligence, we managed to save food and seed grain during years of the grasshopper war. Finally they died off and left the country.

—*Orson Smith*

felt my inability to do the work, but through prayer and study the task was accomplished. A copy was sent to Salt Lake City to the General Board. They accepted and used it in the organization.

In 1875 Father returned from his mission. While in the office I had bought an organ. When Father returned I went to Ogden to meet him and the day we came home I ran in ahead of him and played "Home, Sweet Home." He was happily surprised. Father was a good singer and I thoroughly enjoyed the organ playing and singing. I taught Father telegraphy and we were about a year in the office together.

Barbara Gowans married Benjamin Lewis Bowen on July 24, 1876, in the Endowment House in Salt Lake City. They homesteaded in Tooele, Utah, and became the parents of eleven children. Barbara supported her husband while he served three missions for the Church. She accompanied him on one mission to work with the Indians in Ibapah, in the Deep Creek Mountain range near the Utah-Nevada border. Barbara served as a ward Primary president and member of the stake Primary board in Tooele, loved doing genealogical research and temple work, and was active in the Daughters of Utah Pioneers organization. In 1933, a new DUP camp was established and was named the "Barbara Bowen Camp" in her honor. Barbara died June 3, 1942, in Tooele, Utah.

SOURCE:
Autobiography. *Our Pioneer Heritage* 9(1966):412–22.

Horace Hall Cummings

Born: June 12, 1858, Provo, Utah

Parents: Benjamin Franklin and Catherine Hall Cummings

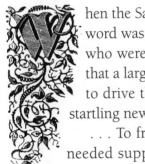

hen the Saints had been in Utah about ten years, on July 24, 1857, word was received by Pres. [Brigham] Young and a large company who were celebrating "Pioneer Day" in Big Cottonwood Canyon, that a large army was approaching the settlements and threatening to drive the Mormons again from their homes. This was indeed startling news!

. . . To frustrate the army and prevent them from getting much needed supplies, Brigham Young ordered the people to take their belongings and move South before the army came. . . . My parents, with the rest of the people, obeyed this order, and long lines of covered wagons wended their way southward, not knowing just where they would finally stop. When father reached Provo mother could go no farther, and the best

I owe my life to an Indian named To Weep. I was out in Hurricane Valley and my horse gave out. I was almost choked to death and I hadn't any idea where to look for water. This Indian rode up and took me to a place where by digging down in the gravel we found a little spring and drank and watered our horses and camped. We slept that night side by side and came home the next day. To Weep Valley is named for him. He was a fine little Indian.

—*John T. Beatty*

Before [the grasshoppers] left they had taken nearly all kinds of crops except peas. People had found out they did not like peas so they all planted peas, all who could get the seed to plant.

—*Caroline Pedersen (Hansen)*

shelter he could obtain for her was old Father Billingsley's granary, where, on a straw bed on the earth floor, I was born.

Some were not so fortunate as we. A cousin of mine was born in the corner of a willow fence that surrounded the lot in which his parents camped, the mother being housed on two sides by the fence, while a piece of carpet formed the roof and another side. . . .

With birth my troubles began, for in spite of all that could be done for me I did not breathe and my skin turned purple and they thought I would never live, but finally father administered to me and I then began to breathe. When [I was] but nine days old a large cat sprang from a beam above me and alighted on my head. Her claws tore such a deep gash across my head that mother thought that I would bleed to death. The scar this left lasted me nearly all my life. In spite of all I grew and thrived, and became an exceptionally fat baby.

The first event that made a definite and connected impression on my mind was this: Long after our short sojourn to Provo, and after we had returned to our home in the north, three big "Indian chiefs," as we called them, came to our house to see father. My father had been on two missions to Salmon River to the Indians and made many friends among the red men, who frequently visited him for counsel or other assistance.

While they talked with father we little ones eyed them with mingled awe and fear, and kept at a respectful distance. Mother went to work and prepared for them the best meal she could, and invited them to dine with the family. They gladly accepted the invitation for no doubt they were hungry and had no such meal at home as was spread before them.

The blessing was asked and the food served. But our guests did not eat. They looked at each other and then at the members of the family. They took up their knife and fork, but did not know how to use these tools provided as their hosts did. They were in a very uncomfortable dilemma and greatly embarrassed.

It happened that at this point a tea kettle, hanging on the crane over the big fireplace, boiled over and spilling water onto the hot coals of a wood fire, made quite a splutter. All heads turned at once to see what was the matter, and while none of the folks was looking at him, one of the hungry Indians seized a piece of meat in his fingers and thrust it hurriedly into his mouth. Alas! The same act that pushed the meat into his mouth pushed his fork, which he had forgotten to drop, into his eye!

He gave such a yell that I was so badly frightened that I do not remember what else happened that day. . . .

In those days food was very scarce and very plain. Nevertheless when people had company

I was baptized north of [Richmond]. [The area] was all covered with hawthorn bushes and known as Muddy River, [and is now called the Cub River]. Several boys were baptized that day. I remember how cold the water was. It took your breath as you waded out into the river to where we were to be immersed. The water came almost up to our shoulders. When one of the boys, LaFayette Tibbets, came up out of the water he said, "Hell, that's cold!" He was immediately immersed in the water again. When he came up the second time, he kept his mouth shut.

—*Rulon Francis Thompson*

One day mother went over to visit one of our neighbors and left [my] brother Harry to look after some peaches, which were cooking in a big iron kettle over the fire, while I was churning butter. The peaches were being preserved in molasses, our only form of sugar in those early days. Harry thought they were done and took them off the hook, but as they were not done and he could not get them back on the hook, I lifted them up over the fire, using my apron as a holder and the flames set fire to my dress. I ran out of the house screaming for mother and running against the wind. The wind fanned the flames but kept them out of my face. Mother came running from the neighbors and beat out the flames. I was in bed for a whole year and was unable to walk for a long time after that. I was told that I would never walk again, but with the help of the priesthood and God, I did walk again. I don't know what all mother used to cure my burns but I remember her paying a lady $6 for two tablespoons of sweet oil, thinking it would help me.

—*Mary Ann Chapple*
(Warner)

they tried to find something a little out of the ordinary to offer the guests to eat. Our tables were small and our families were large, so whenever we had company it was the fate of us little ones to wait until the second table [was set] and eat what happened to be left [over]. . . .

One day mother "had company." While she conversed and seemed to have a good time with her guests, she also proceeded to prepare for them as good a meal as she could. . . .

I . . . remember that as the process of setting the table proceeded, she placed a dish of cucumber pickles on the white table cloth. O my! Cucumber pickles! What three-year-old's mouth would not water at such a sight! . . . I lingered longingly close to that table and wondered if any cucumber pickles would be left for those [of us] who waited. I was doomed to wait, and what could I do?

I do not know why it did not occur to me to ask mother for a piece. . . . I thought to myself: "When my eyes are shut I can see nobody, all is darkness; hence nobody can see me."

With this thought in my mind, . . . I shut my eyes as tightly as possible, approached the table carefully, raised myself on tip-toe, and reached over and secured a small piece of pickle between the tip ends of two fingers. Placing the fragment in my mouth I hastily chewed and swallowed it. When I opened my eyes and put on an innocent look, mother and her guests burst into a fit of laughter which I could not understand. I wondered if big folks could see in the dark.

. . . Not all was sorrow and suffering in those days. We used to coast downhill [on sleds] without the danger of street-cars and automobiles that fill that sport now with fear and danger. Porter Rockwell, or some other lover of juveniles, would often get a long string of boys on sleds trailed behind his sleigh drawn by two or three span of fine horses, and with sleigh bells jingling, and the

happy boys shouting, we would fly over the snow, as he cracked his whip and shouted at his horses, and regardless of the speed limit, would whirl us up one street and down another as fast as the horses could go. And woe was to the luckless urchin who, on turning a short corner at such a rate, was unable to steer his sled and got turned over sled and all in the deep snow at the side of the beaten road.

Stop for him? No, that would spoil the fun! With a loud laugh, in which all the lucky ones who passed the danger safely joined, the crowd rushed by, leaving the luckless one to brush off the snow and hunt his hat and wend his way home.

In summer we played baseball and cricket, and went down to the Jordan River to fish and to bathe. Small boys played . . . with homemade marbles made from native clay and dried in the sun.

One winter my father was not able to get me any shoes, and I had to go barefooted all winter. This meant that I was a prisoner. You can't imagine how long that winter was to me! None of you

Aunt Esther owned a white cow. One evening the cow did not return with the others to be milked. Everyone looked all over for her but could not find her. About dusk Aunt Esther thought she saw a light object coming from the creek bed. Thinking it was Bossie she went toward the object saying, "Co, Boss, Co, Boss." When she went to touch Boss on the head a pair of blanket-draped arms spread out and hugged her close for an instant. She knew immediately that she had mistaken a blanketed Indian for Boss. She screamed and was about to faint when the Indian laughed and let her go saying, "Heap scare white Squaw."
—*Sarah Ann Murdock (Lindsay)*

Why Indians both frightened and interested me, I do not know. They were always kind to us. One day my forearm was lacerated in the cogs of a wringer, turned by the old squaw, Sally. She dislodged my arm, ran to the creek and was back in no time with a poultice of pounded herbs. This she placed on my arm as tears ran down her wrinkled brown cheeks. She called at the house every day until my arm was healed.

—*Cornelia Adams*
(Perkins)

have ever seen so long a winter I am sure. Just to think of a little four-year-old looking out of the window at the other boys going to school, snowballing, sliding on the ice, or having some other kinds of sport, and wishing and wishing he could go too!

But one day my older brother took pity on me, . . . put me on his sled, took me to a hill near our home and let me slide down with him a few times. How I enjoyed it! The big boys would help him haul me up, so I rode both ways. . . . But their goodness finally exhausted itself and the other boys coaxed my brother to go with them to a bigger hill farther away, and they told me to go home. Instead of running quickly around [on] the beaten path, I thought I could save time by going home cross-lots. I found, however, that there was a crust frozen on top of the snow that was not quite strong enough to hold my weight. At each step it would nearly sustain me, and then suddenly break and let my foot go down to the ground to my knees, the rough edges scratching my legs, making them smart and pain me in the cold. I wished I had taken the other route, and I soon began to cry and call loudly for mother.

When I got near enough so she could hear me from the house, she waded through the snow to where I was crying, and picked me up in her arms and carried me into the house, and warmed my feet before the big fire-place.

When my feet got somewhat over the pain of such severe cold, I chanced to look up into my mother's face and saw that she was crying. I wondered why she was crying—she had shoes. But,

O I know now why she was crying so bitterly that day.

. . . We were taught our ABC's [at school] in the old fashioned way. . . . We stood in a group around a teacher, and she would point to one letter after another asking us to name them as she pointed to them. When she would ask the whole class to name them in consecutive order, I could get along, but when she skipped around, I would get their names all mixed up.

One day she got quite out of patience with me because I could not remember the letter L, so she wrote it on the back of my hand with a lead pencil. Perhaps because of her impatience she pressed so hard on the pencil that it almost cut a letter L in my flesh. That time while impressing my hand she surely impressed my brain and I know the letter L to this day!

. . . The city water works consisted of a number of wells sunk from 20 to 40 feet by individuals. If not fortunate enough to own one yourself, perhaps an accommodating neighbor a block away might allow you to drink water from his well. . . . For a year or two I was employed by the Salt Lake Theater to carry water in a large 5-gallon tin can from a well situated on the corner across the road east of the Theater, for its patrons to drink between the acts from a tin cup which all used.

We small boys used to enjoy [our mother's] quiltings very much. [We loved to] lie on the floor under a quilt suspended on quilting frames . . . and listen to the chatter of half a dozen sisters doing the quilting. . . . We would . . . snicker at their expostulations. [Our] fun [was] almost equal to our anticipations of the good dinner that

One Sunday father and mother went to conference and left my sister Alice and me at home to play in the yard. All at once we [saw] a big buck Indian coming up the sidewalk. We were terribly frightened so we ran in the house and got under the bed. It was an old style bedstead, what was called a four-post bedstead. It had curtains around it; so under the bed we went. We thought we were safe, but in our hurry to get under the bed we forgot to shut the door as we came in. After we had been there it seemed to me a long time, I poked my head from under the curtains and there stood that Indian with his arms folded, looking right at me. Well, I do think I would have died with fright if it had not been for a good neighbor, Nancy Haws, who saw the Indian come to our house and knew father and mother had gone to church. So she came to our rescue, took me in her arms and tried to comfort me. The Indian just laughed and tried to make friends with us, but I was too frightened to look at him. I have never forgotten that incident although it has been fifty-five years ago.

—*Rachel Elizabeth Pyne (Smart)*

One time when I was returning from school in the first ward there was a little girl [who] came along wearing a red hood. There was a slaughter house about 33rd street below Washington Avenue in the center of a field. This little girl's father was a butcher and his name was Wright. He had a wild Texas steer they were going to slaughter and it got out of their control and jumped the fence and was running down Washington Avenue. Two cowboys on horses were trying to catch it and I happened to be walking along about where the little girl [with the red hood] was and I told her that she had better get off the street until they had caught the steer but she said she wasn't afraid. About the time that it got even with us it made a dive right for the little girl. I was so frightened but I managed to grab the little girl under one arm and with my free hand I jumped over a board fence around a house and just got into the house as the bull broke the fence and got in the yard. He sure was wild and they were compelled to kill it right on the street.

—*John Clements West*

always followed. Sometimes we would amuse ourselves [by] counting the number of times the busy quilters would change the subject of their conversation. Once we counted up to 42 and then quit!

When [I was] only about ten years of age a man named John W. Morehouse, a wealthy mining man, moved into the house next to ours and hired me to work for him, paying me $10 a month and my board. I slept at home. I did the chores and most of the family marketing.

. . . Many times I have had to carry home a huge basket so full of meat and vegetables that I had to set it down on the sidewalk to rest every few rods. Sometimes, when it was necessary to buy a hundred pounds of flour . . . I would borrow a neighbor's wheel barrow and wheel it home.

At the end of each month, I gave my wages to my mother, and the thought that they were mine never entered my head. Therefore, it was no sacrifice. I realize now [how important] that small salary was to my mother, for we were very poor.

. . . [After] we all moved back to Salt Lake into our home in the 12th Ward, I . . . got work for our Elder's quorum in the Salt Lake Temple Quarry. The President of the Church had called on the different quorums to furnish at least one man each to work on the Temple, and the work was progressing rapidly.

. . . Physically, this was the hardest work I had ever done. Great granite stones as big as a house were cut into blocks by drilling a row of holes five or six inches deep and as far apart, along a line of cleavage, putting into each hole two slips and an iron wedge, and tapping each wedge in turn with a hammer, a mighty pressure would be gradually developed that would finally split the huge stone along the desired line. The two halves would then be cut into blocks of stone of suitable size and shape to be shipped and dressed to fit into certain places in the walls of the Temple. They were loaded onto the [railroad] cars at the quarry and delivered at the Temple Block where they were properly dressed and laid in the walls.

Little did I dream when I was splitting those huge stones in the hot sun on the mountain side that I would live to see that magnificent Temple dedicated and receive all the ordinances given in it, and then . . . be called with a number of my family to be regular workers in it for many years!

I worked in the quarry about eight months. This gave me . . . valuable experience, and the physical exertions each day developed my muscles and did my body good. Besides helping father, I saved up enough for my tuition at the Deseret University—about $40, and enrolled at the end of the first term.

. . . However, I had to discontinue at the end of the third term. My father and oldest brother had both been called on missions and I had to quit to support the family.

So I quit school and began to look for work. . . . There was little to be found. . . . I visited the stores, the shops, the trunk factory, the railroad, and even tried to find work on nearby farms. I would have been glad to get $1 a day doing any kind of work. Night after night I would come home with no prospect of work, until I began to feel very discouraged. The baby was sick and

[I remember] the sight of the great stones one at a time being hauled along the streets by two yoke of oxen [for the building of the Salt Lake Temple] and we would all stand for them to pass with a feeling of awe and reverence.

—*Annie Wells (Cannon)*

In the summer much of my time was spent in Little Cottonwood Canyon, and there I watched the men digging and blasting the great granite blocks and preparing them for delivery to the [Salt Lake] temple. I can remember the days of the ox teams and how they tugged with their heavy loads, and how at intervals down the canyon road rough-cut blocks had skidded from the wagons and were lost.

—*Joseph Fielding Smith*

Daddy was a blacksmith. There were about 150 Indians in West Weber at the time. They were always friendly and the Ute chief liked father and father told him if he came over some day he would make some iron points for his arrow. The Indian returned in a few days and Daddy made the iron arrow points for him. The Indian was very pleased and told Daddy that he would bring him a goose soon. He brought the goose and he had evidently shot it on the fly as the arrow had gone nearly through it. He patted father on the back and said "You white man, I like you." We often found flint arrowheads and other Indian relics on our farm but we didn't think anything of them at the time but I wish now we had saved them.

—*Lorenzo Hadley*

mother was not very well and the stock of provisions was getting decidedly low, and I began to feel that something must be done.

. . . [One] morning . . . I came into the kitchen where mother was and found her crying, and concluded that she was worrying over our diminishing stock of provisions and poor prospects for more. Without asking any questions I went back into the closet in the new house, closed the door, and knelt in prayer. . . . I had a peculiar earnest determination to get what I wanted. I prayed with so [much] earnestness that I cried.

I fear that my prayer was somewhat of a complaint, for I told the Lord that He had called my father and brother both to preach His gospel and left me to support the family; that I had looked and looked for work and could find none, and that I did not think it was fair. I must have work.

After relieving my feelings in this way, I waited there in the cold until I thought the redness had gone out of my eyes, lest some one might ask me what I had been crying about; then I ventured into the room where mother was.

To my surprise there sat two school trustees talking to my mother. It seems that they wanted a teacher in their district and had come to town to get one. After a short conversation they engaged me at $60 a month, and to begin at once!

The Lord so prospered me that by the time father got home from his mission, I had the new house completed and all paid for. As soon as we got the roof on and the walls plastered, mother took in boarders and in that way helped considerable. Thus my prayer was more than answered. The Lord prospered our family for obeying His call. Also that is the way I happened to become a teacher, and last, but not least, that is the way I happened to get a wife.

Horace Hall Cummings kept a journal from the time he was thirteen years old. A schoolteacher by profession, he married Barbara Matilda Moses (who was a student in his classroom) on August 4, 1881. They had seven sons and two daughters. Two of their children died as infants. Horace served a mission to Mexico from 1885 to 1887, acting as mission president from May to October 1887. He married a second wife, Matilda Sophia Wilcox Bliss, on April 13, 1890. He taught at the University of Utah and later served as general superintendent of Church schools. Horace died August 1, 1937, in Salt Lake City.

....
SOURCE:
Autobiography. Photocopy of transcript. LDS Church Archives.

The great event that I shall never forget was when the Indians came through [Farmington] on their way to their fall hunt. They always came from the south. They would be strung out for miles, a few old squaws in the lead, then would come a motley string of all kinds, all on horses. Most all the horses would have large packs on their backs with women and children riding some of them. Tent poles were tied to some ponies with the ends dragging bedding, cooking utensils, and papooses piled on.

The grand sight was the Indian men. They wore buckskin trousers and jackets, feathers in their hair and their faces painted. They sat on their horses with such grace and dignity. They carried their rifles lying across the saddle in front of them. They would camp north of town and stay two or three days, but no one but a few old squaws would come into our town. They came to beg for "biscuits" as they called our bread. The others shunned the village. They were the Lords of the prairies and a happy carefree people.

—*James T. Bigler*

Catherine Heggie (Griffiths)

Born: March 4, 1867, Clarkston, Utah

Parents: Andrew Walker and Annie Thompson Stewart Heggie

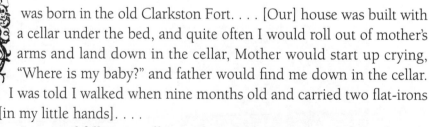

was born in the old Clarkston Fort. . . . [Our] house was built with a cellar under the bed, and quite often I would roll out of mother's arms and land down in the cellar, Mother would start up crying, "Where is my baby?" and father would find me down in the cellar. I was told I walked when nine months old and carried two flat-irons [in my little hands]. . . .

It seemed falling in cellars and water ditches was a failing of mine. When I was about three years old, I used to fall in the water ditch in front of our house. Dave Quigley, a neighbor boy, saved me from drowning two or three times. His father used to tease me about it, and tell me when a man saves a lady from drowning he was supposed to marry her, he would say. . . . I used to dislike him so much for teasing me that I would run and hide every time he came to our home. Mother was so worried about my falling in the water she decided to send me to school for safe keeping. I started to school when about four years old. Betsy Griffin was my teacher, she used to punish me by tying me to the table leg with her apron strings. . . .

My childhood home as I remember it, was one log room with a small window in the east side, a door in the north end, with a dirt roof, there were log beams with willows then straw and dirt on top. . . . [When] we had a bad storm we would sometimes wake up to find pans strewn over our bed to catch the water as it dripped through the roof. After the storm the walls would be stained with yellow streaks where the water had leaked through the roof of straw and earth, this made more work for our mother as she would not rest until she got it white-washed and cleaned the room up again.

We all wore home-spun clothes. Our parents had a small flock of sheep. I remember seeing Mother preparing the wool to send it to Brigham City to the cording mill. . . . [I] used to help pick the wool, for which she would give us children an egg each, and we would trip off to the store for candy. It was hard tack, there were fish, elephants, dogs, bottles, and such was the candy we got in the early days. . . .

Sometime after moving to our new home I would go with my sister Annie to herd sheep on the bench back of town, we would have some jolly good times, as everybody used to dig Segos to eat. We played marbles and ball.

Often in fruit time, [the Indians] would gather a pan of chokecherries or service berries

We took up some land [in Richfield, Utah] and lived in a dugout. I drove the ox team while my brother John plowed the ground to plant wheat. Many a time while driving the team, I fell down, tripping over greasewood, scratching and hurting myself until I cried.

When the ground was ready to plant all the people took their wheat to the schoolhouse and a prayer meeting was held. God was asked to bless the seed wheat that each kernel might grow and stool out, bringing forth abundantly that we might have bread to eat. Our prayers were answered and we had a good crop, threshing it with flails.

—*Eva Christine Beck (Zimmerman) (Harrison)*

I remember one summer it looked like the crops were all going to be destroyed by grasshoppers. They came in swarms and settled on everything green. Fields, gardens and orchards. Everyone—men, women and children—turned out to fight them. Trenches were dug and we drove what we could into them, where they were burned or covered with dirt. It looked like everything would be destroyed. Then one day when there was a celebration being held over in the old bowery (I think it was the 24th of July) we noticed it looked like a cloud over the sun. On looking closer we found it to be the grasshoppers taking their leave. What rejoicing there was. The crops were saved.

—*Julia Hanson (Hall)*

to sell to Mother. They were so pleased when our baby brother Willie would go to them, they would pick a large cluster . . . and give them to him. The next summer they came again with fruit and asked for "the little papoose," and when told he had died they were very sad and shook their heads from side to side.

Father's team was named Ret and Flora. Flora had fought in the Indian war before Father got her. You could always tell when Indians were in town by the way she would prick up her ears and snort and prance around the corral trying to run away. We girls, my sisters Annie and Sarah and myself thought we would have a ride on Flora as she was very gentle when there were no Indians in town. Annie put Sarah and me on her back and was leading her around the yard. As we went round the house our brother and cousins had made a wigwam out of wagon bows and a wagon cover. As we went past one of our cousins sprang out and yelled. This frightened Flora, she reared and threw us off on the hard path, knocking us both unconscious. We were soon revived and Mother told our cousins to go home and not to come back, but we were soon playing together the same as if nothing had happened. . . .

I was baptized August 8, 1875 by Martin Harris, Jr. . . . There was a large crowd as some were getting baptized into the United Order. There were a number of covered wagons strewn along Big Creek just south of Big Creek Bridge east of town. I was baptized for the remission of sins and into the United Order at the same time. I remember Emily Jane Homer was being baptized and she gave a scream and threw her arms up, and one arm was still dry, so they had to baptize her the second time. I was confirmed by Andrew McCombs the same day.

When a small girl I attended Sunday School Jubilee, held in Logan in a Bowery. President Brigham Young was there and a great many of the children went and shook hands with him. When we were coming home, Bishop Rigby's horse got scared and jumped off the bridge into the Bear River. The bridge was not safe so the people had to get out and walk across. We were all frightened. Bishop Rigby's girls were crying and wringing their hands, afraid their horse would be drowned. They cut the harness and guided him to a safe place to get him out. It held up the whole company, as they were the first to cross the bridge.

The first part I ever took in a play was when my school teacher, Frank Miller, gave a school exhibition. The name of the dialogue was "The Imps of the Trunk Room." Rebecca Homer and I had parts. We as youngsters got into an old trunk and dressed up in old time clothes. She as a lady and I as a gent with a sword. Then we took a high chair and dressed it up with hoops and old time clothes with slippers peeping out from under the dress and a broom sitting up with a head and face drawn and an old time hat. We were dancing around it and along came an older sister and thought the room was haunted and while [she] was gone to hunt investigators, we slipped out of our duds, jammed

One time my mother had baked two lovely loaves of salt rising bread and had left me alone while she went to a neighbor's. Soon after she had gone a big Indian chief came into our house. "I want bread," he said. I was afraid, but I told him, "You have one loaf and me one loaf." "No, me two loaves," and saying this he pointed his bow and arrow at my face. I told him to take them and ran to the neighbor's where my mother was, then fainted dead away.

—*Alma Elizabeth Mineer (Felt)*

[Indians] very often came to our house. Father was very good to them and they loved him. If an Indian is your friend he will remain your friend and do anything in his power for you as long as he can trust you and you never break a promise to him. They had their wickiups down there and I remember one of their papooses died and they came over for father to take it up to the cemetery and bury it there, and father did.

"Little Soldier" was their chief and he very often came to our house for breakfast. He was very religious and wouldn't sit down to eat until he had asked the blessing and he would pray for quite a while, asking our Heavenly Father to even bless the cattle on the hills and everything he could think of. When "Little Soldier" died, father and Frank Rushton, and a Mr. Gale made his coffin and dressed him. They dressed him in his temple robes as he was a member of The Church of Jesus Christ of Latter-day Saints.

—*Mary Elizabeth James (Jones)*

them into the trunk and skipped. When they came back, the room was all straight.

Soon after this Susannah Clark taught me to step-dance. "The Highland Fling" and "Sailor's Horn Pipe" which I used to dance between acts in the dramas and entertainment. We used to help to raise funds for different organizations. The dress I wore for dancing was a short full skirt, low neck, short sleeved white dress with rosette soft pumps with red ribbon laced around my legs to the knee. My hair was in ringlets and a wreath of artificial roses. I later made a Scotch Highland Kilt for dancing the Highland fling.

We children were brought up in a religious home. It was a rare occasion that we ever missed a Sunday School or meeting. I remember the only time I stayed home from meeting. The other members of the family had all gone to meeting. I stayed in the house for some time until I got scared of the silence. Then I went for a walk around the lot. I was frightened there too and began to wonder if I would be killed by some tramp or some other harmful person. I was sure glad when the family got home from meeting. I never wanted to stay home alone after that experience.

My courtship days started in an unusual way. Will's [William John Griffiths] step-brother, Samuel Thompson, bet him he dared not ask me to go to the dance with him. I was clerking in the co-op store and he brought some wheat to buy his ticket. He watched his chance and when the store was empty of all shoppers but him, he asked me to be his partner to the dance. He asked and of course I accepted and he won the bet. If I'd known it was not [out of] admiration for me that he wished my company I doubt whether I would have consented or not. As it was he continued to escort me to dances, sleighriding parties and home from Writing School, night meetings and such. I was about 13 years old.

He took me to a circus in Logan, and what a treat that was to me. It seemed I was in a fairyland. Then he took me to a theater, "Uncle Tom's Cabin" in Logan. This was one of the greatest treats of my life.

Our first falling out was when he took some whiskey with the boys at a dance. I refused to have anything more to do with him. He wanted to explain he only took a swallow, but I would not listen. So we parted for a time. Our next falling out was when he decided to get even. So he just left me without any explanation. It seemed we were at outs for good, until he decided there was no other girl he wished so much for a companion through life, and I had made up my mind there was no other man for me. We continued our courtship until we were married January 6, 1886, in the Logan Temple.

Catherine and Will became the parents of eight children, six of whom lived to maturity. Catherine supplemented their farm income by

When fruit became very plentiful and we had more than we could do ourselves, we would gather a good many bushels and pile them up on the ground, then invite all the young folks in some evening to a "cutting bee," we called it. Some would cut and carry [the fruit] to the scaffolds in baskets made of water willows and then those on the scaffolds would spread the fruit on the boards. I have seen whole wagon loads of fruit cut and put out in just a few hours that way. Then after the fruit was all done we would play games and have refreshments, most generally all the watermelon and grapes we could eat.

—Alice Ann Langston
(Dalton)

When I was twelve years old I took my father's mules and wagon and went alone after a load of wood up the Santa Clara. A lone Indian spied me and seeing I was a young boy and alone, jumped upon my wagon and demanded that I give him some bread. I took my bread sack and started to untie it to divide with him when he suddenly grabbed the whole sack and attempted to climb off the wagon. But I grabbed the bread sack with one hand and succeeded in pushing him off the wagon with the other. I then took a large black whip which I carried for the mules and quickly lashed them into a gallop. The Indian hung to the back of the wagon trying to get my ax free from its keeper so he could strike me with it. But every time his hands came up I would [strike] them with the whip. He followed the wagon for a short distance until he became exhausted and then gave up the chase. I continued on my way and returned the next day with a good load of wood.

—Isaiah Cox

boarding schoolteachers. She was active in Relief Society, sewed burial clothes for the dead, and served as captain of the local chapter of Daughters of Utah Pioneers. Her husband died in 1934, leaving her a widow for the last thirty-four years of her life. She died April 14, 1968, at the age of 101.

SOURCE:
Autobiography. Photocopy of transcript. Utah State University Special Collections.

PART THREE

Extending Zion's Boundaries

lthough the Salt Lake Valley was the main arrival point for immigrant families coming into the Utah Territory, it was not the end of the journey for many of them. Some weary travelers barely had time to wash up and enjoy a few meals at a real table before they were on the road again to a more distant settlement.

The Saints established hundreds of new communities throughout parts of what are now Idaho, Nevada, California, Oregon, Wyoming, Arizona, and Utah. By the end of the nineteenth century, in fact, some 325 permanent settlements had been founded in Utah alone.

Families volunteered or were called by Church authorities to settle these new communities, a task that required resourcefulness, patience, and the ability to work together. In addition to building homes and establishing farms in remote areas, rugged pioneers of all ages worked together to build fences, canals, roads, telegraph lines, and railroads. They established blacksmith shops, the silk industry, woolen and flour mills, tanneries, and boot and shoe shops. As new communities were born, schools, meetinghouses, cooperative stores, irrigation systems, and theaters sprang up throughout the Great Basin.

Young persons contributed significantly to these ventures. They planted acres of farmland, fed and tended livestock, learned to spin, sewed burial clothing, thinned sugar beets, produced cheese, learned telegraphy, taught school, carried the mail, and drove heavily loaded wagons through sometimes treacherous terrain.

The contributions made by youth to the settling of the West are only beginning to be understood. To read of the mountain of work they accomplished, even at very young ages, is to comprehend that Mormon youth were valuable partners with their parents in building up the promised land.

Martha James Cragun (Cox)

Born: March 3, 1852, Mill Creek Ward, Salt Lake County, Utah
Parents: James and Eleanor Lane Cragun

Martha is shown holding a child in the above photograph.

had not arrived at the proper school age but went [to school] as a visitor with my older brothers and sisters. But as I learned nearly the whole alphabet that day my parents thought it well to let me go continuously thereafter since it was summertime. One incident only impressed my mind for always. 'Twas of a boy hanging by his feet from one of the joists in the room—his face red and eyes bulging. This was given as punishment for some unruly act. My wonder afterward was how the teacher, she being a woman, ever got him up there. The children were all crying for fear he would fall. . . .

My brother Elisha, older than myself, had amused himself by twisting the curls of a little girl who was sitting in front of him on one of the long rude

I disliked washing dishes. . . . The water was heated on the top of the stove and we used a dishpan to wash the dishes in. We had a bar of homemade soap to put in the water and most of the time before the dishes were done the water was cooled so much that the grease collected around the inside of the pan in a ring. The water had to be thrown out into the yard or kept in a "swill" barrel for the feeding of the pigs. We had to wipe all the dishes as there were no sinks and dish drainers in our homes at the time.

Making the beds we used was really difficult. There were no fitted sheets nor innerspring mattresses. We removed all the quilts, blankets, and sheets then stirred up the straw in the tick till it was loose and smoothed out even. Then we replaced the bedding, tucking it in well all around. We then put on the bed spread and pillows. . . .

[Twice a year] the old straw was emptied from the bed ticks which were washed, dried and refilled with fresh straw. It was lots of fun to roll on the carpets with their soft cushion of straw and climb onto a bed with a well-filled straw tick.

—*Ellis Day (Coombs)*

benches furnished for the primary classes. The teacher's attention was called to the offense and she decided that his own hair should be burnt off as penalty for his act. [I believed the teacher meant what she said and was not teasing.] She ordered him to bring chips from the wood yard and place in the stove that stood in the corner. All this he did with a grin on his face. He was bidden now to kneel down and blow up the imaginary fire. But when he was told to put his head into the stove that his hair might be burned off—I grew frantic. I ran to the teacher, clasped her knees and begged for mercy for my brother. The loud laughing of the school children made the scene demoniacal. It was sometime before her assurances would quiet me. I was shown the dead embers in the stove. I was shown the stove pipe that had been taken down and now stood in the corner behind the stove. When the act was all over I was too weak to stand. And at night I suffered from delirious fever and frightful dreams. The teacher was not censured for her folly—but I was laughed at so much for my foolish frenzy that I would go no more to that school.

The next summer another English lady came to teach our district school. She was a very proper lady and "preached decorum," which . . . most of her pupils tried to observe. As they entered school in the morning they were required to give salutation to her by a low bow from the boys and a curtsy by the girls. On one of my first days at school—it may have been my very first—I seemed to be unacquainted with the regulations. I walked right in without noticing my preceptress. She looked at me and said in a kind voice "Where is your [curtsy] dear?" I stood there puzzled to know what part of the school paraphernalia I had left behind. She repeated "I want your [curtsy]." Then I answered very timidly, "Oh, I didn't bring it with me."

The following winter was a severe one. The snow fell deep. My mother could not make up her mind to let me walk a mile and a half to school during the severe weather. Besides my brother Elisha was very sick for many weeks, which occupied her time and she needed me at home she said. Many in the neighborhood were sick and many healings were granted by the Lord through His Holy [Priesthood]. My brother was given his life through this power.

All day I remember, my mother wept behind the old fashioned bonnet she wore. In the evening my father brought in the Bishop with his counsellors and said, "Brethren I have brought you in to ask a favor of the Lord for me. I want you to administer to my boy who is very low." They went to the bed and prayed over him and laid their hands upon him and promised him life. The next morning while we were eating breakfast two sisters of the ward called. They hesitated at the gate. When my father opened the door they advanced timidly and said they had come to enquire about the boy. They had heard he was dead. I remember my mother saying to them: "Here he stands. The Lord has been in this house." He stood in an inner doorway combing his hair, and looking so pale and thin with eyes so large. I shall never forget the picture. I formed the idea then that the Lord loved my father very much and that the priesthood held mighty power.

I did not have places to go and play when a child, but stayed home, and as soon as I was old enough I had to help with the work. I had to do a boy's work as well as a girl's. I herded sheep and cows, worked in the field, helped load the hay and thresh the wheat. I helped my mother weave cloth and did the general housework. One time I bought a blue glass egg-cup and a little glass salt dish with wheat I had gleaned. I tromped on the heads of the wheat, then blew the chaff away and sold the wheat. I wove a white blanket when I was fourteen years old.

—*Sarah Doney (Hatch)*

One time when I was quite a small girl my aunt Clarrissa Terry told me if I would get lucerne [alfalfa] for her pig all summer she would weave me a dress. Every day when I would go to take the pig feed I would torment her by asking "Is that my dress?" She kept me waiting until the last of the piece. Then came out a many colored striped cloth for a dress. Was I proud? Well I think that was the first thing I ever earned.

—Julia Hanson (Hall)

There was another remarkable case of healing during that winter, that of Moroni ["Rone"] Casper. . . . Our father was asked to call at the Casper home to administer to the boy. He found the father standing at the gate weeping. The [doctor] had just left after saying that Moroni could not live but a few days longer. "He does not need to die," said my father. "The Lord is the one to decide and not the doctor. He is the Lord of life and death." My father went in and administered to the boy. When he came out he told Brother Casper to not admit the doctor again because [the doctor said the boy would die. . . . He said to admit only those who had faith that the boy would live]. Then he gave him this charge "Send word to the children in school that just as soon as Moroni gets well enough you will give them a party—a ward party—and treat with candy and raisins." A party for the children—unheard of except once a year a little dance on Christmas afternoon. Oh how the children prayed for that party. At home no parent was allowed by the children to forget to pray for the recovery of "Rone." Prayers for the boy ascended night and morning by every family of the ward. At school during recess the children assembled in groups in the brush to pray for their schoolmate and went singly many times a day to offer their petitions. My sister M.E. says she prayed for the boy five or six times a day. It might seem a strange story to some but the prayers of the children prevailed and when the boy was able to be out again the party was given. . . .

[Martha's father was soon called to help settle Southern Utah's "Dixie." They spent the summer in Pine Valley, moving later to St. George.]

The summer in Pine Valley was sweet to me. . . . I felt that God was good to make a world so wonderful for us to live in. [But] our frail open shanty was no protection from the cold icy winds and snow [of winter]. We children had to retire early to our beds where I would lie and dole out the long evening hours listening to the howl of the coyotes on the nearby hills and the hum of my mother's spinning wheel as she spun in her wagon box. . . .

Oh, the long nights. I could not go to sleep early. I found a way to open the cover of the wagon box just a little way. I practiced an imitation of the coyote howl until I could fool the coyote himself. Through the opening at the head of my bed I would thrust my face and emit several howls. It would be answered immediately and soon I could see their dusky forms flitting over the snow. But their having one night gobbled up one of Tisha's cats (which I threw out into the snow because of its persistency in sleeping on my bed at night) killed my [interest] in them. I never called them again. . . .

We moved to St. George in November [1862]. . . . I loved to dance and almost any kind of dance was better than none. They were usually noisy affairs. The boys wore heavy boots and the shoes of the girls were not such as fairies wear. The floor was swept at intervals. . . . All took part in the waltz. The straight forward waltz—none of your clasping close and young ladies reclining on the bosom of the young men. The good cotillion

Our first clothing was made out of cloth that was much thicker than canvas. It was so thick that holes had to be punched with an awl to sew it. When the girl's dresses were made they would stand in the middle of the floor alone. It was anything but pleasant to wear shirts and trousers with seams as thick as your finger, especially with nothing underneath them. I was twenty years old before I had my first ready-made suit of clothes.
—*John Staheli*

None of [the children] had shoes but wore muskrat skins that had been salted and dried and they tied them on their feet.
—*Mary Elizabeth James (Jones)*

In those days, we hardly knew what shoes were. My feet were so calloused and tough on the bottom that mesquite thorns and cockle burrs would hardly penetrate them. If it happened to be in a rocky place, and after dark, my feet were so hard and tough that when I stubbed my toe, I thought I saw sparks flying. The Carpenters were real tenderfeet, and when they would come to cockle burr patches which they had to cross, I would carry the big Carpenter boobs one by one, on my back, across the cockle burr patches, until the last one was across. They would actually pile the cockle burrs up to see me tromp on them.

—*Edward Maddocks Claridge*

we had—the reels and the "money musk" and the schottische and the polkas. . . .

On Christmas eve [1862] a tall gawkish young man from Pine Valley called to see if he could get a partner for the dance. My sister M.E. was already engaged to go, but in sympathy for the young man, I suppose, she told him that I would accompany him. When she told me what she had done I was so angry I deluged her with abusive epithets for presuming to dispose of me in such a manner and without my permission. But mother came to her aid, and reasoned with me. . . . I repented and we all set off together. The inspiration of the music of one violin and my love of dancing soon chased away all [un]comfortable feelings. . . . The evening I think would have been a perfect leisure but for the fact that some of the Belles of the party made fun of my partner. This I could have borne though had not my sister joined in their jests of ridicule. Then I hid myself in shame in a corner by the fireplace and behind the onlookers. . . . When the ignorant fellow went out with the mischievous boys and took too much whiskey I could not keep my tears back and I stole out unobserved and ran home to have a good cry. I never quite forgave M.E.

One night [while my father and mother and two younger sisters were in Salt Lake City] my brothers were both absent. It was never intended that I should be left alone at night and [I] had never been without one of them there but an unexpected circumstance detained them from home. The evening gave promise of wind and storm. When a child, I always cried when the wind blew and I had not yet overcome the weakness entirely. Tonight the [swaying] of the pine tree that shaded our hut sent a sickening feeling to my heart. I went out into the yard to survey the heavens that were gathering black clouds. Down by an old work shop I saw an Indian. My first thought was that he was a spy or scout for a party on a raid, but he had no gun and his limbs were naked. . . . I concluded he was a common Indian seeking shelter and I knew he would freeze in the open roofless shop. I went to him and told him to come to my wickiup and [get] warm. He said "St Wino, Tic a boo"—meaning "Good. I'm your friend." I gave him some supper and a seat by the fire where we two sat together till late in the night. While the worst storm the ranches ever knew howled terribly outside and fairly shook the old cabin, I felt so thankful for the company of that dirty ragged Indian in the dilemma of the storm. And he was grateful for the storm. He told me his tribe had cast him out for some very bad thing he had done and some wanted to kill him. He would say the wind and snow were good because they could not find him nor track him. . . . Tomorrow he would be away over the mountain. I asked the Indian if he had killed someone. He said no, that killing was pretty good, that he had done worse than killing. There was a little "lean to" behind the cabin into which an inner door opened. I showed him an empty corn bin and told him to lie down in that when he wanted to rest. When the storm abated he went into his rest and I laid down on my cot

When I look back on it now, I wonder how we ever got along and would not [have], had it not been for the Saints living near us. Although they had but bare necessities, yet each was willing to share his or her little with those less fortunate.

Mother traveled to Salt Lake City, a journey of three or more days there and back, to get our first sugar. It was brown sugar and carefully hoarded in a sugar bowl with a cloth tied over it, to be used only on special occasions, generally when company came. We children got very little of it. Sometimes when mother went to Salt Lake City, she would bring back a few canned goods. After we used the contents, the rough edges of the cans were melted off and then polished up to be used as dishes or utensils. I can remember standing over the tables, especially when we had company, waging a switch keeping the flies from the food.

At the time the family was suffering the most from lack of food, clothing and shelter, mother received a letter from her father. He offered to send her enough money to take her back to Scotland, but she refused.

—*Jane Sprunt (Warner) (Garner)*

We stopped . . . for our dinner with an old friend of Mother's named Hawes. She had warm biscuits and fresh butter. I nearly mortified my mother to death by buttering both sides of each half of the biscuit about a half inch thick. I was reprimanded for it. The old lady laughed heartily and said, let him put on all that he wants to, there is plenty of it. We had not had much butter that summer and I was pretty hungry, especially for warm biscuits and fresh butter, and I still like both.

—*Francis Adelbert Webb*

before the fire and went to sleep. When I awoke I found he had gone. . . . When it became known [the] next day that I had braved a stormy night alone (for I would tell none of them about my Indian) my reputation for bravery was somewhat redeemed.

In this year of 1865 [when I was 13], . . . mortality among the children in the Dixie settlements . . . was very great, actually appalling. Not a week of that long summer but someone either child or an old person was taken to the graveyard. The young people took an active part in filling the office of night nurse. Death had an awful terror to me, and nothing, it seemed, could induce me to touch a corpse. . . . This caused me many times to try to shirk my duty when asked to sit at night with one who was expected to die. But I had my lesson to learn, and it was effectual.

My mother sent me one evening to the home of a poor widow to enquire about her sick [baby] and with instructions to remain the night with her if she needed me. The baby was worse, she told me. She asked [me] to sit by it while she took a little rest. After sometime had passed I perceived the child was dying. It was an awful task to me to call the mother to see her baby die. I [agreed] to go out at her request to call in her neighbors but was held in check at the door by their dog, a large fellow who had been howling on the steps for sometime and who seemed to have suddenly become fierce, and [he would not let either] of us go out.

The time we sat by that dying child seemed very long to me, while the dog never ceased to howl. When it was all over, the mother asked me if I would . . . perform the next sad rites. I could not refuse as there was no other way.

The mother completely worn out with her long nights and days of watching and caring for her little one laid down with her other children on a ragged bed in the corner and fell into a sleep. I did the best I could but suffered under the ordeal. . . . When I had washed the little fellow and wrapped him in a piece of an old white window curtain I laid him out on the flat top of an old chest. By this time the only candle the widow had was burned down and it began to flicker and then flare up for a moment as the spirit of the little child had seemed to do and then fell down and went out forever as he had done. There was a pan of chips by the fireplace and these laid on the coals one at a time kept the little light I needed to sustain my reason. I dared not look at the dark door-less hole that led from the room into the cellar underneath the floor. This reminded me so much of an open grave.

The wind blew hard and rattled the windows and whistled thru the openings in the chamber above. . . . During the short intervals in which the wind seemed to lose his breath I could hear the mice or rats scampering on the floor above making the dust fall down on my head. It was with the utmost economy that I made my chips last through the remainder of the night. As

Mother used to send me to the neighbors, Mrs. Kapple, to get yeast to make her bread. I would [take] a little bucket with a cup full of sugar to Mrs. Kapple's home, get it filled with yeast and start back to our house. But before I got home about a third of the yeast disappeared. I just loved to drink it. Mother never questioned me but I am sure she knew what had happened.

—Martha
  Jane
  Miles
  (Edwards)

Just before Christmas once I wanted to earn some money to buy presents and tried to sell children's books. I went to one home where there were six little children ranging from 8 years to a baby a few months old. The mother was holding the baby trying to keep it warm; none of the children had shoes on and the fire in the stove was not enough to keep the room warm—it was so drafty. So I just left one of the books and hurried home, telling my mother that I could not ask people like that to buy books where I was sure they were hungry. Mother told the Relief Society and helped fill a basket to take to them. I shall always remember how this poverty affected me.
—*Martha Jane Miles
(Edwards)*

daylight appeared the dog left his post by the door. The wind and the rain ceased. The shadows of the night departed and a glorious morning was ushered in. I could afterward assist in the care for the dead without the feeling I had had before.

Martha married Isaiah Cox December 6, 1869. They became the parents of eight children, two of whom died in childhood. To help support her family, Martha taught school every year but two when she was between the ages of seventeen and sixty-nine. Once, finding the schoolhouse unfinished in Muddy Valley, Nevada, she taught "under the beautiful cottonwood trees by the side of the lovely clear stream," using her black-painted breadboard as a chalkboard. Martha spent her last years performing temple work in St. George, Manti, and Salt Lake City. She died November 30, 1932, leaving a valuable, hand-written autobiography of more than three hundred pages, written in 1928.

SOURCE:
Martha James Cragun Cox, "Biographical Record of Martha Cox: Written for My Children and My Children's Children, and All Who May Care to Read It." Holograph. LDS Church Archives. Typescript available at Utah State Historical Society and at Brigham Young University.

James Martin Allred Sr.

Born: March 30, 1865, in Salt Lake City, Utah
Parents: James Franklin and Jane Thompson McKenzie Allred

I was born of goodly parents in Salt Lake City, March 30, 1865. When I was about eighteen months old we moved to Wallsburg, Wasatch County, [Utah]. In 1866 [on my journey there] my Mother carried me over a big snow slide in Provo Canyon. . . .

What little schooling I got was in a little one-roomed log school house. There was about 75 to 100 students taught by one teacher. I never went after I was fourteen years of age.

I herded cows in the summer time bare-footed among the rocks and [prickly] pears and rattlesnakes. My parents were very poor. With a large family to feed and clothe, they couldn't [give] us but one pair of . . . copper-toed boots in the fall to wear to school. Talk about hard times. . . . We hardly ever saw a dollar in cash. Our only resources were hauling lumber, logs, poles, wood

The first apple I ever tasted was one of a box George Q. Cannon sent mother from Salt Lake City. I took a bite from mine every day for a week until it was gone.

—*Ann E. Melville (Bishop)*

There were three big boys on the farm: Jim, Tom and Wayne. I used to sleep with them in the loft over the house. We spent one Christmas Eve at their house and we all hung up our stockings. The stockings were all full the next morning. The boys gave me some of their candy and it tasted like their feet smelled, but I ate it anyway.

—*James William Nielsen*

and railroad ties to Provo and the other lower settlements and trade them for store pay, factory pay and sorghum.

During the summer of 1879 Utah experienced one of the worst droughts in history. There was nothing raised to speak of and the feed dried up on the ranges and in the mountains. Even the grass was so parched and dry that our oxen couldn't get half they wanted to eat in the fall after a hard summer's work. So therefore it was necessary for all of us through Wasatch and Summit counties to take our stock to winter range. So my Father was hired to take the Wallsburg stock to the Uintah Reservation for the winter and he took me along with him to help drive to the range and be company for him.

When the snow began to get deep in those high lands we drifted down the country towards the mouth of Strawberry River and made our winter camp right where Duchesne City stands today. We found plenty of good feed . . . and our cattle and horses came out fat in the spring.

I want to relate one circumstance that took place. . . . Joe Owens and I, both of us boys about fifteen years old, were hunting cattle in that region and were coming back towards camp. . . . We saw a lot of Indians coming and they saw us about the same time. Here they came as fast as their horses could run keeping in the edge of the cedars on the side. When they got even with us they surrounded us and said, "Are you White men or Mormons?" We were mighty glad to tell them we were Mormons, so they didn't molest us further and we got off with a good scare.

. . . Back [at] our winter camp, in February, the ground was dry and dusty. We made a race track and the Indians came to run races with us. Billy Preece had two or three race horses that we thought were very fast. The Indian horses had also wintered out and their hair was long and looked shaggy, the men thought they had a cinch. The Indians were eager to bet on their horses and the White men covered everything they would bet, but when the races were over the Indians walked away with all the spoils and there were some sad looking cowboys as they went back to their camps that night.

About the middle of April, . . . we were getting right down to cases on food. By this time my Father and Mr. Owens thought it best for Joe and I to go home and send some men with a supply of food out to help them in with the cattle. So Father made us each a pair of snow skis out of cedar and took us to the head of Deep Creek on horses. . . . The snow was at least six or seven feet deep, not a thing to burn to keep us from freezing. . . . We climbed up and managed to find enough wood to keep us warm by wrapping up in our quilts. The next day we got on our way and that night found us in an old sawmill cabin in Daniels Canyon. We were ravenously hungry and in searching [through] every nook and corner we ran across a little flour and some lard, no

In 1861 father was called to Dixie. I remember the days of preparation . . . before leaving. Mother and my sisters, Emily and Abigail, spent days making crackers. They mixed them and pounded them with a wooden mallet. They dried corn, squash, berries and tomatoes. It was as if we were going into a wilderness expecting to starve. When it was time to go, a big double bedded government wagon was brought around to the front of the house. It had a bed in each end with a stove in the middle and a chair for mother. It had a ladder down from the door in the center and the kiddies climbed in and out while the wagon was going to walk a while or climb in to get crackers and then [they] got out and walked a while. There were three yoke of oxen. All the relatives and friends mourned and carried on and expected never to see each other again, as though we were going into the wilderness never to return.

[Along the way] we camped a few nights in deep snow where men had to shovel snow for a campground and cut trees for a shelter. We landed in Toquerville about the last of November, [and] found a summer climate, cotton still in the pod on the bushes, Indians gathering beans, and seeds of all kinds.

—*Hannah Adelia Bunker (Crosby)*

I recall Ogden's first lighting [ceremony]. A steel pole was erected on 24th Street hill a little above where Ogden's old court house now stands. There was installed on this pole a light that was described as being so bright that citizens of Ogden within the boundary of a mile and a half or two miles would be able to read a news-paper under its brilliancy. Ogden's Band turned out for this special occasion. All mem-bers of the band wore caps which had small lamps upon them to furnish light for them to read their music by. They did not remove these lamps off their caps for this occasion. Everyone anxiously awaited this great event, but after the light was flashed on, it was very dim and proved a great disap-pointment to the people of Ogden. In fact, it was so dim, the members of the band had to light their little lamps on their caps in order to play their music.

—*T. Samuel Browning*

baking powder, no salt. But oh boy, didn't we stir up some scones and baked them on top of the stove. . . . I'll say we were rich. We made it home to Wallsburg the next day all O.K. We hadn't heard one word from home all winter and when I got within about one mile from home I met an old neighbor by the name of John Parcell. He began telling me of the children that had died in that little Burg [Wallsburg] during the winter from diphtheria. I thought every second he would tell about some of my brothers and sisters dying, but thank the Lord there were none of them seriously sick with that dreaded disease. When I got to our front gate Mother met me and said, "Martin, you mustn't come in as some of the children are in the worst stage of the disease."

Then mother told me there had been 32 chil-dren die there during the winter, as many as five in one family. I was only fifteen years old, hadn't seen Mother all winter long and was so homesick to see the rest of the family. I wanted so much to take her in my arms and hug and kiss her, but she wouldn't even shake hands with me for fear of leaving a germ and I might be exposed. You can imagine my feelings at that moment and also hers.

While [Mother] was thinking and wondering where I could go or what I could do, . . . a man rode up to us on a beautiful black horse. It just happened to be our old friend John McKeachnie who had come down from Park City. . . . He had a cord-wood contract and was . . . delivering his wood to the Ontario Mine. Mother told him our troubles and he said, "If you will let Martin go with me and cook for my men I will give him a dollar a day and board." Mother decided that was the best and only thing for me to do. So I had to leave home again for another 2 or 3 months.

When the diphtheria cleared up I was permitted to return home and Oh Boy, wasn't I a tickled kid. I never can forget the joy we all had at our meeting, and to make it more pleasant Father had arrived with the stock all O.K.

Martin married Margaret Lindsay Camp April 6, 1887, in Grand Junction, Colorado. Their marriage was solemnized some years later in the Salt Lake Temple. They became the parents of thirteen children. Martin helped to establish the Uintah Basin by building roads, canals, and bridges, some of which are still in use today. He served as justice of the peace and director of the Central Canal Company. He also enjoyed church service and held callings in various organizations. Martin died April 30, 1953, in Salt Lake City, and is buried in Vernal, Utah.

SOURCE:
Autobiography. Typescript. Utah State University Special Collections.

I commenced serving one night every week as a guard at President Young's office. . . . There were from eight to twelve always on duty at the President's office every night. As a rule one at a time armed with gun or revolver was outside the office marching around the premises, challenging every suspicious looking character he saw, opening gates or calling the regular turnkey out to do so when any one had to pass in or out; and the others inside the office, sitting around chatting or reclining on the floor, ready for service at a moment's warning.

President Young would frequently come into his office in the evening and converse for a while with those present and I always enjoyed hearing him, and I think I would not have hesitated about risking my life any moment in his defense. Naturally, of course, those who thus served became more or less acquainted with President Young's home life and that of his grown-up sons and daughters and especially with the young men who were paying court to the fine bevy of girls in the family who were then of marriageable age. It not infrequently happened that the young people wished to be passed in or out, sometimes surreptitiously, and when the guard felt that it was all right to favor them, it was done, and nothing said about it.
—*George Cannon Lambert*

Morgan Jesse Rich

Born: January 20, 1868, Paris, Idaho
Parents: Charles Coulson and Harriet Sargent Rich

The month of January [1868] was a cold, stormy month. Mother was to give birth to [me], her eighth child. Father had been called to Salt Lake City by President Brigham Young and was much worried about my coming. Father was worried because mother had not been in her usual good health.

I was the smallest, scrawniest specimen of the whole Rich family. On father's return he looked at me with grave concern, then comforted my mother saying: "Never mind, Harriet, he'll live." He took me gently into his arms, blessed me and gave me my name. The rest of the winter was hard on both mother and me because I did not develop as her other children had.

When summer came I would creep out of the house every time I found the door open, and leaning against the wall, pick bits of lime from the daubing and eat them. When father caught me doing this, he had with him Brother Warren Sirrine. Father picked me up and said: "This will make him sick." Brother Sirrine said: "put him down. He knows what he wants better than you do." After that mother fed me slaked lime rock diluted with water and I began to grow, until the whooping cough came along and I got it. It appeared as if I were dying. Mother sent for father. He administered to me and ordained me an elder. I became well. Although I never grew as tall as my brothers, I was as full of mischief as any of them.

One day when I was old enough to understand, father took me in private and explained that when he ordained me an elder in my infancy, he did so that I might hold that Priesthood in the Eternal World, but since I did not die I would be ordained according to the pattern.

I grew to boyhood and was able to hold my own with my brothers. There were eight of us

Flour was twenty-five dollars a hundred, and as we had no money, many months passed that we had no bread. I well remember how glad I was to herd oxen all day Sunday for other people for a piece of white bread for my pay.

A great part of our time was spent in making molasses during the fall and early winter months. Having the only mill in town we had to work almost continually day and night. I often became so sleepy and tired I could hardly work. On one occasion I asked Father if I could go to bed when the roosters began to crow. About twelve o'clock I began crowing which started the roosters in the neighborhood to crowing, so Father told me to go to bed.

—*John Staheli*

The toughest meal we ever had was an old hawk. I had been out hunting all day and couldn't find any greens or game, but coming home I spied an old hawk perched up on an old stake. I crawled up close to him, as near as I could. I fired and down he came. I took him home and my sister said, "Harrison is this all that you could get?" I told her yes so we prepared him for the pot. When supper time came my sister went to take him up out of the pot but he was so tough she could hardly stick the fork into him. We had to put him back into the pot and boil him the greater part of the night. However we managed to eat him the next morning.

—*Harrison Sperry Sr.*

about the same age, two from each of the four families living in Bear Lake, and father insisted that we all work together and not drift apart. I got in a lot of trouble by doing the mischievous things the other boys told me to do, which usually got all of us into difficulty, but I generally got the blame.

One day father very strictly told us to hoe the weeds from the potato patch, and not come to the mill. He said that if we disobeyed he would "lick us like five hundred."

The mill was a two-story log structure. The machinery was run by a small water-powered turbine wheel which was in the building. We were fascinated by the power of the wheel which turned the machinery that crushed, elevated, sifted, and distributed the flour, shorts and bran. We loved to play in the wheat, and to us that mill was an ideal place to play hide-and-go-seek.

After father had been gone for some time, we dropped our hoes and held a conference. We decided to rest from our hoeing, go to the top of the hill opposite the mill, and see if father was still there. Arriving at the hilltop we could see no signs that would indicate father's presence. He had been so stern that we decided to play a safe game. Cuts were made and the one drawing the shortest was to go down to the mill. If he found Father there he was to walk down the road as if nothing had happened; if not he was to wave his hat. I drew the shortest cut and went hesitatingly down the hill. As I arrived at the front of the mill father came to the door, saw me and said, "Wait a minute. I want to see you." I knew that I was in for it and I knew that the other boys should be, so I stepped out where they could see me and waved my hat. The gleeful group came running down the hill to enjoy the victory of their careful planning. I could never forget the look on their faces when they saw father, nor the twinkle in his eye when he saw their startled expressions. When he was tickled but could not laugh there was a little quiver on one corner of his upper lip. Yet true to his word he lined us up according to age and gave us the promised "five hundred" and then sent us back to the potato patch. Well, I again got hell from each of my brothers. My hoeing that afternoon was a pretty tough job, for every time I would let up, one of the boys would throw a clod of something at me.

[That] night . . . there was considerable silence around the [dinner] table. Finally Alvin said to me: "I'll bet you won't do again what you did today." Then the whole story came out and father turned to me and said: "You did the right thing." Father was kind to his boys, and we loved to be with him. He often took me to Bern or to his other ranches in the Bear Lake Valley.

One day father took his younger sons to one of his cattle ranches and allowed each to select a cow to be his own. When it came my turn, although I did not know it, I chose father's favorite. Father said: "Since Morgan has the good judgement to pick the best he shall have it." He [also] took me where his horses were feeding and allowed me to select a mare. I did. She was well-trained. I loved her. She was my pride and joy.

Father always encouraged his family to attend to their Church duties. Well do I remember the

When I was nine years old, mother [sent] me to [live with] Uncle Beason Lewis. For some time I had not tasted bread. I was hungry. Cooked wild roots and weeds were my bill of fare. When Uncle Beason took me to his house, Aunt Betsy cut off a big slice of bread, spread it thickly with butter and gave it to me. That was the sweetest, best food I ever ate in my life.
—*William Lobark Skidmore*

During the [Primary] organization meeting Sister [Eliza R.] Snow showed us a watch which had been the Prophet Joseph's. She told us about the Prophet and the watch. She let each of us hold the watch for a short time. I remember as I held the watch in my tiny cupped hands, she gave us an admonition not to ever forget that we had held the Prophet's watch. . . . I imagine the rest remembered as I shall always the story Sister Snow told us of the Prophet and the wonderful moment when we held his watch.
—*Violet Lunt (Urie)*

After [Father and] Mother's death my sister and I . . . moved to Orderville and joined with the other Saints in living the United Order. We had our own living rooms and shared alike in all things. At meal times we were called by a bugle to a large room where we all ate together. There were neither rich nor poor, those who came with little were helped to get a good start. We lived this way for about eight years. While living the Order we were taught to make our own clothes, shoes, yarn for stockings and mittens, scarfs, sweaters and caps, tanned our own leather, raised everything we ate, owned our own grist mill and a large spinning wheel. We also had many sheep and cattle.

—*Florence Ellen Fowler (Adair)*

Sunday when I returned from Sunday School and learned that father had [suffered] a stroke which caused him to be an invalid for three years. He died November 17, 1883.

Apostle Moses Thatcher was the main speaker at my father's funeral. I stood by Elder Thatcher and held his gloves while he knelt down and dedicated the grave of this GREAT PIONEER.

From there on my mother had the care of her ten children. Hard though it was, without the counsel of her beloved husband, she became equal to the task. As the years passed, my brothers and sisters were married, and I was left alone with mother. We became very close to each other, so close that I did not care to go out nights but remained home with her. At this time she told me her life's story bit by bit. . . .

[*Morgan soon received a call to serve a full-time mission for the Church.*]

I arrived at Chattanooga, Tennessee, which was the headquarters for the Southern States Mission. My brother, Ben E. Rich, was the mission president. He assigned me to Virginia. My first companion was Leslie George. It was here in Albemarle County I began my missionary labors as the greenest, most homesick country bumpkin you ever saw. The food was not as my mother cooked. I shed tears, got blisters on my feet, and was no good to myself, or to the Church, for I was always longing for the time when I could go home. One day while traveling through the woods I stopped and said to my companion: "This thing has got to be tested. You sit down by my grips [bags]. I'm going into the woods and have a talk with the Lord." I found a secluded spot at the trunk of a tree, and this was my prayer: "Oh Lord, I'm homesick and you know it. I want you to remove that feeling so I can stay and fill an honorable mission. If you don't I'm going home. Amen."

I went back to my companion, shouldered my grips, and said: "We're ready to go." That homesick feeling left me, and I made friends wherever I went. Passages of scripture came back to me in astonishing numbers. I traveled without purse or scrip, enjoying to the full the blessings attending missionary work.

Morgan served two missions for the Church, one to the Southern States and one to Great Britain. He married Sarah Elizabeth Bradley on August 17, 1910, in the Salt Lake Temple. They had four children, two of whom died very young. They lived in Paris, Idaho, where Morgan enjoyed working as a flour miller in the Paris Roller Mills, which his father had built. Morgan was a counselor in the bishopric and also served as Sunday School superintendent for eighteen years. His greatest sorrow came in 1920 when his wife and their two-year-old son died within two days of each other during an influenza epidemic. Morgan died July 28, 1951, at the age of eighty-three.

....

SOURCE:
Autobiography. Photocopy of transcript. LDS Church Archives.

They used to hold their annual fairs in the large rooms of the Tithing Office which was a large building. They were supposed to have all homemade products. I was representing a homespun girl. I was dressed in cloth made in the valley from my skin out. I wore nothing imported except the thread that my clothes were sewed with. No buttons or hooks or eyes were on my clothes. Instead they were fastened on with thorns gathered from brush in City Creek Canyon. I, of course, had to walk around through the rooms for inspection. I took first prize.
—*Mary Louisa Woolley (Clark)*

There was a great scarcity of bread stuff one year. The grasshoppers took the grain one year and the drought one year and the hailstorm one year, which caused quite a famine in the land. We had to live on pigweed greens and young beets and mushrooms with some milk and butter. My father had a fat blind ox which he took up north and his gun. He sold the gun for one hundred pounds of flour and the ox for 25 bushels of good potatoes. While my father was gone up north a lady gave me a loaf of bread for combing her hair. I was so hungry that I could hardly wait until I got home with it.
—*Hannah Isabell Fawcett (Nixon)*

Mary Elizabeth Woolley (Chamberlain)

Born: January 31, 1870, St. George, Utah

Parents: Edwin Dilworth Jr. and Geneva Bentley Woolley

nlike [my sister] Minnie I was very plain and unattractive, with small "squinty" blue eyes, straight, coarse, dun-colored hair, with a "cowlick" so it never would part in the middle. Thus I started life handicapped from the beginning, but Mother would apologize for my looks by saying, "Well, she has a sunny disposition anyway," and for that one endowment I have been very grateful, as it has been a greater asset than looks possibly could be.

My first photograph I well remember. We had a fine vineyard at the back of the house, of which Father was very proud. He picked the largest bunch of California grapes he could find and took Minnie and me down to Jim Booth's to have our "pictures took." We wore dresses of blue and grey plaid linsey and Mother had arranged a bow of blue ribbon on my hair to cover up a few of its defects, but when we posed for the picture, standing behind a chair with the bunch of grapes hanging in front, Father thought the dress looked too plain and needed a sash; so he proceeded to take my hair ribbon and tied it around my waist. It barely reached around me and tied in a hard knot. It looked like a white carpet rag in the picture, much to Mother's disgust, when the pictures were finished and delivered.

I was a member of the first Primary organized in St. George. . . . I still have a copy of the first Primary Hymn Book which was published soon after the organization. It is a small book, with no music; but, oh, how I love those songs!

I don't remember paying tithing in my very early childhood, but we were taught to save every cent we got and donate it to the St. George Temple which was being built at that time.

Father made Minnie and me a little bank by taking a small pasteboard box, covering it, lid and all with wrapping paper, and sealing the edges so we could not possibly get into it. Then he cut a slit in the top for us to drop the coins in. Pennies were not in circulation at that date, so it was nickels and dimes, and I do not remember ever spending one for candy or useless toys. . . .

When the [St. George] Temple was nearing completion and our bank was opened, we turned over to the Bishop $2.50, our life's savings!

After the St. George Temple was finished, we began the same thing for the one at Manti, so "saving" was my middle name, and I have carried it all through my life.

As before stated, I was a very plain and unattractive child, large for my years. During the adolescent period I was as shapeless as a sack of meal

There was an older lady, Margaret Shaw, who lived on the corner south from us [in Provo]. She taught me to knit and how proud I was with my first pair of mittens I had knit. She would tell me about the Prophet Joseph Smith and Hyrum and the Saints in Nauvoo; how she had seen the room where the Prophet was killed and the blood stains on the floor; how she had listened to him preach with such power and how the mobs abused him and his brother Hyrum. I would sit and knit and listen by the hour and it made a very strong impression on my young mind.
—*Rachel Elizabeth Pyne (Smart)*

We used to make our hats, for in those days we didn't have the money to buy them. After the wheat was harvested, my mother would send us kids out with sheets that we laid down on the wheat stubble. We would take scissors and clip the straw along the ditches and other places where the harvesters had not gotten it. We would lay it evenly on the sheets, then four of us would take the corners of the sheet and carefully carry it home. We would cut the heads off the wheat to feed the chickens. Nothing was wasted. We would then make the hats from the straw by splitting, soaking, and braiding it, then sewing it into the shapes we wanted. After the hats were finished, they were bleached with sulphur fumes to make them white. We made fine hats and they were considered real nice.

—*Lydia Merrell (Goodrich)*

tied in the middle and had extremely large feet. Oh! How I have suffered with humiliation, time and time again, when "Uncle Dan" [Seegmiller] would pass remarks about my awkwardness, or call attention to my big feet, which were usually covered with homemade cowhide shoes, which did not lessen their size nor add to their beauty in the least. He always seemed to take delight in teasing me and many times I have left the crowd and cried myself to sleep in humiliation.

I remember several times while we were in Salt Lake [City] . . . we rode on the little old mule-drawn street cars, with Brother Crabtree as driver and conductor. How those poor little mules had to pull! When they got to the end of the track they stood on a sort of turn table, which revolved and got them started back again. I was also in Salt Lake when the first electric car was run.

On February 7, 1878, I was baptized by my father, Edwin Dilworth Woolley, Jr., in a little pond just north of the old 4th Ward school house in St. George, and confirmed by Henry G. Platt on the same date. It was a cold, raw day, which I remember distinctly, as there were no accommodations there for dressing and I had to ride home in my wet clothes a distance of several blocks, but I felt no ill effects.

In the fall of 1876 I entered school for the first time in a little one-room adobe school house on the brow of the foothills north of town, known as the 4th Ward school house, and used for Sunday School as well as day school. There were no grades then, so one teacher had to supervise all pupils from beginners up. They ranged in age from tots of six to grown up young men and women, some of whom were taller by far than the teachers. I remember the first lesson on the chart and can see it now, in big black letters, as the teacher pointed with a long, slim, round stick to each word, and we read, or rather drawled in concert, "I see a fly! I see a fly! Up, up he goes into the sky. I will not hurt the fly. No, no, little fly, bye, bye."

After I was old enough to say my prayers, away from Mother's knee, I would often forget them, sometimes for several nights, and then when I did think of them I would say them over and over and over, to pay up, always being sure that I repeated them enough to have a few times left over for interest so that the Lord would forgive me.

. . . The first letter I ever wrote was to a dear playmate, Minnie Romney, who with her father, Miles P. Romney, and his family, moved to St. Johns, Arizona. Mother thought it was not worth the postage, but Father said it was good experience and I would never learn if I did not practice on someone, so he gladly furnished the stamps for that and many, many others, as we carried on a regular correspondence until we were grown.

In the spring of 1881 an epidemic of diphtheria broke out in St. George and Aunt Flora's little brother "Bertie" was one of the first to die

I lived with my parents in Springville seven years and I remember the hard times there. One winter we had to ration; my father and two older sisters gleaned twenty bushels of wheat and had it ground into flour which had to last all winter. Mother would make small biscuits and we could each have two a day. Mother said after times were better we still wanted our two biscuits.
—*Lovenia Nicholson Sylvester (Berry)*

If we got a pound or two of sugar in a year we were lucky. I remember my mother saving a pound of sugar so she would have something nice to eat when her baby was born. Now even though there are only my son and I at home, I never think of buying sugar in anything but 100 pound sacks.
—*Laura Smith (Hadfield)*

When I went across the plains I got my first pair of buckskin pants. I got them about the first of March. I went up into the mountains the day I put them on and it snowed and they got wet and stretched until I had to keep rolling them up. They lasted all summer and until I came back from across the plains.

—*James J. Adams*

We had only one decent dress at a time, so we had to go to bed early Saturday night so Mother could wash not only our dresses, but all our underwear too and dry it through the night that we might be clean for Sunday. But I never remember hearing my mother complain.

—*Sabra Jane Beckstead*
(Hatch)

with the terrible disease. They did not quarantine nor fumigate . . . and as a result her little daughter, Evelyn, or Eva as we called her, took the disease and died on May 8, 1881. This was a terrible blow to all of us, as we loved her so dearly, and she was such a beautiful child.

Aunt Flora was broken hearted and so lonely that Father took Minnie down to the field to stay with her for company. She took the disease, and after suffering untold agony she died June 23, 1881. This was awful! The memory of it haunts me yet! After Minnie's death I was indeed lonesome, as we were always together, always dressed alike, and were almost like twins.

Father took me with him whenever possible, taught me to hitch up and unhitch the horses, how to drive the team, which line to pull for "gee" and "haw," in fact, everything that a boy of that age should know. He always wished I was a boy and trained me as if I were one. When I was eleven years old, he put me on top of a load of hay and had me drive the team from the field home, a distance of six miles or more, and through the Virgin River, which was full of quick-sand—and really dangerous. My heart was in my mouth 'til I was safely over it. He drove one team and went ahead and kept one eye on me 'til I was over. It was dark when we arrived home and I thought I was quite a hero.

In thinking over the economies of those days, I remember seeing one lady rip up an old dress to make over for one of the children. She picked out the stitches one by one and saved the thread to restitch it with. Another incident is told of a family who was at supper and the little brother called out, "Ma, Jake's wastey! He picked a fly out

of the molasses and never licked its legs off." And "Wastey Jake Beecham" was a byword throughout the town for years, and still is in our home.

We blackened our shoes with the soot from the bottom of the stove lids or the back of the fireplace. The brush was dipped in water and rubbed over the lid. On special occasions a little molasses was mixed with the water to give it a better shine. We were never fortunate enough to have an extra pair of shoes for best, so on Saturday night each pair, including Father's boots, had to be blacked and made ready for Sunday, and the task usually fell to me. I do not remember a box of shoe polish in the house 'til I was at least twenty-five years old, and then it was not the perfected article we have today. . . .

When one of the neighbor children was sick with putrid sore throat [diphtheria], . . . Mother went with [Dr. Israel Ivins] at night and carried the lantern while they searched through the lots and up and down the water ditch to find a frog, which he cut open and bound on the throat, thus saving the child's life. Mother never would let one of us kill or mistreat a frog or toad after that.

[In the spring of 1882, Mary's father was called by Apostle Erastus Snow to move to Upper Kanab, Kane County, Utah, to take charge of a ranch and dairy owned by the Church.]

This [move] was a great trial to Mother as her health was very poor, she would have no neighbors nearer than half a mile, no social or educational advantages for the family. Her parents were getting old, and she dreaded to leave them as it seemed to her that she was going clear out of the world. She cried and cried for weeks before the move was finally made. Elder Snow, learning of

Bluff, [Utah] is surrounded by high cliffs and there are cracks in the rocks where one may hide or walk as the case may be. One occasion I well recall, a group of us boys went for a hike and climb. The older boys went on ahead of Dill Hammond and myself because we were the youngest of the group and slower. After having reached the top of the rock, the older boys started rolling large rocks down off the cliffs and they would become lodged in the cracks. The older boys got through [on the way down] but Dill and I couldn't make it and were terribly frightened. My brother Corry who was with the group, suggested that Herbert Redd kneel down and pray for us, presuming Herbert had more faith and was a better prayer. So they gave Herbert a nickel and he prayed and immediately we were able to get down. This is one of the many instances of the efficacy of prayer in my life.

—*Daniel Perkins*

her grief, visited her and promised if she would stop grieving and go willingly that her health would improve and that she would never regret the move, and this promise was more than fulfilled. Her health gradually improved until she was well and strong, and able to work as hard as anyone of her years. She adjusted to the ranch life and was a leading spirit among the neighbors for miles around who made up the community.

The milking of the cows night and morning was quite an affair. The milkers, which included boys and girls, had to be up before the sun. In fact, we had to be up almost as soon as it was light, so the task could be completed before the flies began to bother and the sun got too hot. Each cow was named, some after individuals, both men and women, of whom they reminded us, either in the expression of their faces, disposition, size, form, voice, etc. It often sounded ridiculous to onlookers, of whom we had many as the seasons came and went, to hear us call to the calf runners to turn out Napoleon's or Madam Patti's calf. . . . Many of our near neighbors, or friends in St. George, were honored with a namesake. I milked an average of twenty cows night and morning every summer as long as we ran the dairy.

In the evening after the milking and other chores were done, we would gather and listen to

There was one poor cow which we milked and we thought considerable of her. [She was lost.] I spent quite some time looking for her. When I found her, she was so poor and weak she couldn't get up. I got off my horse and tried every possible way to help her up, but she was too weak to get up. I stood there worrying over our losses and seeing this poor cow, so I went over a short distance from where the cow was lying and knelt down and offered a simple prayer to the Lord that He might bless the cow so that I could get her home. After I had prayed I went over to where the cow was and spoke to her (and not to my amazement because I had faith in what I had supplicated for) she got up and I drove her home a distance of four or five miles. Please do not smile at these child-like prayers, they are very sacred to me.
—Daniel Perkins

Aunt Mishie sing and play on the little old organ which was a prized possession of those days. Some of the songs I remember were "Ben Bolt," "When you and I were young, Maggie," "The Bridge," "Silver Threads Among the Gold," . . . "Tenting Tonight" and many other . . . popular songs of the day, besides Sunday School hymns. Those were great times in our young lives and how we did enjoy them.

About this time Uncle Dan went to Arizona to work on a railroad then being built by John W. Young near Flagstaff. When he returned, he brought a great big old fashioned stagecoach. It had three seats and a trunk rack on the back. We used to hitch four horses on it and load it to the brim. The driver and grownups in the seats and the children standing in between and lovers holding each other on the rack behind—and off we went to Sunday School, dances, picnics, or wherever there was to go. Quite the envy of our neighbors less fortunate. We always went as fast as the horses could trot and sang at the top of our voices as we went.

While I was [visiting] in St. George Father was very anxious for me to take music lessons and arranged for me to do so from old Sister DeFreize, a typical English lady of the old school and a very good teacher. He promised to buy me an organ as soon as I learned to play a tune, so I proceeded with all diligence.

I had music in my soul but it was hard to get it into my fingers, as they were used only to sweeping, scrubbing, washing, milking cows, etc., and they were not lady fingers to begin with. So it was quite a task and required almost more patience than I could muster. I persisted,

In the fall of 1854, when I was seven years old, I needed and wanted a new dress badly. One day while I was playing in the yard I found an old bacon sack and took it to my mother. She made some lye water by soaking wood ashes and in this she soaked the sack to remove the grease. Then she got some weeds and made dye in which she dyed the sack brown. From this she made the waist and from a piece of blue denim the skirt, and I had a new dress. How proud I was of it!
—*Melissa Jane Lambson (Davis)*

Father was hired by the railroad to paint their locomotives. In order to be with him, we moved to Evanston, Wyoming for two years. The winters were bitter, and the snow often fell so deep that we had to dig our way out of the house. I remember milking the cow when long icicles hung from her nose and almost freezing my hands when milking her.

—*Mary Ann Chapple (Warner)*

That first winter [1857] I earned my living as a cowboy. I was only 12 years old. Jim Larkin and I were out on the range at Clinton and Hooper and we herded a lot of cattle that Lot Smith had taken away from Johnston's Army in Wyoming. . . . It was mighty cold at times out there on those desolate flats along the lake shore. When we were hungry we would ride up to a cow that had a calf and milk a nice stream of hot milk into our mouths.

—*Samuel Banford*

however, and finally wrote Father that I could play "The Corn Flower Waltz," "Nearer My God to Thee," and one or two other simple pieces. He was so delighted that he ordered the organ at once and had it sent to me at St. George so I would have it to practice on. And oh! Wasn't I proud!

[The organ] was a beautiful instrument, a Kimball. When I returned to the ranch [in Kanab] the organ was packed and sent, too, and what a gala day at home when it was set up in the front room and I proceeded to show off my talents—ha ha!

But, alas! It practically ended there, as there was always so much work to do. Mother offered to do all the work if I would only practice; but she was not strong and could not do half that needed doing, and when she sent me in the front room to practice for an hour, I would find the organ covered with dust, and children's clothing, playthings, etc., scattered over the floor. . . . I could not sit down to practice 'til the room was set to rights, dusted, etc., and by that time the hour was up and I was called to other tasks. Thus it went day after day 'til I finally forgot what little I knew.

[Abia E. Johnson] was my first real love. We "kept company" all during the winter [of 1885–1886]. Abia came up every weekend during the summer. The little boys, Jode and Roy, used to entertain him while I was busy, by telling how they had to toe the mark when I was around, how I scrubbed and cleaned and "swept the path clear to the barn" when I knew he was coming . . . etc., and etc.

One evening we were sitting cozily in the

front room when Roy, age eight, came in swinging the "lariat," stating that he was going to lasso Abia's nose, much to the latter's embarrassment, as it was a very prominent feature.

[In the fall of 1889, the Woolley family moved to Lower Kanab, so Mary's father could more easily take care of his duties as the new stake president. This also enabled the children to attend better schools and associate with more friends their own age.]

There was no hotel in the town and we were about the only ones who had a spare room, and it was usually occupied. We never knew what it was to eat a meal alone, and the best of everything was always served for company.

We entertained all the General Authorities of the Church, including the representatives of the auxiliary organizations who visited our stake conference for twenty-six years, and even longer than that.

Also, lords and noblemen from England, senators, congressmen, governors, Colonel Cody (Buffalo Bill) and party, railroad officials, drummers, post office inspectors, the exploring expedition of Benjamin F. Cluff and party to South America, of which my brother Royal was a member. They stayed sometime and fitted out from there. We also hosted cattle buyers, sheep and wool contractors, land commissioners and surveyors, artists, sectarian ministers, and novelists, including Zane Grey and others.

Very little remunerations were received . . . but I feel that we were well paid with the opportunity of contacting such characters, which was an education in itself and a privilege that few others have enjoyed.

Being the "[Stake] President's daughters" was

All the girls in Lehi [Utah] could spin. We had a large log meeting and schoolhouse. The Bishop told the girls they could take their [spinning] wheels there and spin. Sometimes more than a dozen would spin at a time. We would talk and laugh—perhaps talk of our beaus. We would spin 40 knots or 12 cuts a day—we tried to see which could get done first—then go home, get supper, do a few chores, then often the girls would go for a walk. We were afraid to go outside of the wall for fear of meeting Indians, so we would take a walk around the Fort and pass close by every door and stop and talk. So you see, we did not get lonesome.

—Elizabeth Zimmerman
   (Lamb)

Noah Avery was always held up before me as an ideal boy by my Mother. She said to me "Noah Avery chopped every stick of his mother's firewood before he was seven years old, and it is almost impossible to get you to chop what little I want, and you are nearly eight." I mortally hated to chop wood and pull weeds. I got my legs tingled with a willow more times for running away and not pulling the weeds than for all the other crimes I ever committed.

[When ten years old] the first job that took me away from home for any length of time was herding sheep for ten dollars a month, and board was included. I am sure I never suffered so much with any kind of trouble as I did with homesickness while on that job. I was never so overjoyed with anything in my life as I was when I reached home. I hugged my mother and kissed her, the same with my sisters. I then sat down and cried and cried. I bawled right out loud. My sisters were very much alarmed and tried to find out my trouble; Mother knew my trouble, and it made her cry to see my grief or joy. I have heard of people crying for joy. I am sure one of those people.

—*Edward Lenox Black*

not as easy nor as pleasant as some may think, for everything we did and said was watched and criticized, not constructively either, at times. If the "Woolley girls" did anything, it gave all others a license to do the same, so that we had to be constantly on our guard, and while we never did pose as being superior in any way, we were expected to be an example. Other girls could say and do things out of the way and no notice was ever taken of it, but let one of us side-step the least bit and the whole town knew about it. When bloomers and divided skirts came in style, I was the first to don them in riding horseback and was criticized severely for being so unwomanly.

Old Brother Charles Cram appeared before the stake presidency at one of the council meetings with a complaint that "Mamie" Woolley had disgraced the town. They all gasped and wondered what ever was coming, and when told to proceed, he said, "Well, Sir, she rode down the streets of Kanab, Sir, straddle of a hoss [horse], looking like a spread eagle, Sir!!" They all gave a sigh of relief, and a hearty laugh, and told him he had just woke from a Rip Van Winkle sleep.

[Mary writes a description of Saturday, January 4, 1896, the day President Grover Cleveland signed a proclamation admitting Utah into the Union.]

The greatest day Kanab has ever seen is just closed. Never were humans more enthused than the inhabitants of this remote burg when they learned that they were full-fledged citizens of these great United States.

Early on Saturday the 4th great crowds gathered around the telegraph office, eager to hear those simple, yet all important words: "Grover had issued his Proclamation." Every urchin in the village was "armed to the teeth" with something to make a noise, ranging from guns and cowbells, to tin pans, wash-tubs, brass kettles, etc. and etc.

When the message came at length, the din which burst forth made the valleys tremble and the hills resound. Nor did the patriotism wane with that day, but as Monday the 6th dawned bright and clear, the artillery aroused each and everyone from his slumbers and as the sun appeared in his glory the national emblem was proudly raised with Utah's brightest star attached.

The Martial, Brass, and String Bands filled the air with strains which aroused the patriotism of every man, woman and child. The streets were thronged with people to witness the procession. . . .

After parading the principal streets of the town all assembled at the Social Hall, which had been beautifully decorated for the occasion, and where large tables groaned under their heavy weight of delicious viands [food].

After five hundred people had feasted 'til they were more than satisfied, the tables were still well filled, and the Indians were invited in and allowed to help themselves. They

too rejoiced in the fact that Utah had at last received the distinction she deserved.

At 4 P.M. a meeting was held. After singing

The houses [in Park City] were made of wood and built so close together that when a fire started it was a serious thing indeed. Both mills would blow their sirens so loud it was terrible. One morning, in January, 1896, just as I was getting dressed, the sirens started to scream. I ran outside with only one shoe on, through the snow, down the steps, across the bridge, and into the store where Father had already gone to work. I must have been a sorry sight, with my uncombed hair flying, shoe untied, etc. Everyone in the store laughed at me. It was not a fire nor the end of the world, but the noise was because *Utah had become a state!*
—*Regina Mary Simmons (Christensen)*

It had been such a long time since I had any shoes, that at eight years I hardly knew what they felt like. It happened that one day as I was helping mother lift a heavy tub used for washing our clothes, I let go of my end and the tub fell on my bare toe. My toe was almost smashed and when Mr. John Gillard, a shoemaker, saw it, he promised me that if a lady didn't call within six weeks for a pair of shoes that he had made for her little girl, he would give them to me. How I prayed that the lady wouldn't come for the shoes, and she didn't. On the sixth week, Mr. Gillard brought me the new pair of shoes, the first real shoes I had since coming to America.
—*Mary Ann Chapple (Warner)*

"Utah the Queen of the West," prayer was offered by one of the early Utah pioneers.

Enthusiastic and patriotic speeches were made by both ladies and gentlemen (I being one of them), all of which were received with deafening applause from the densely packed audience.

After giving three cheers for "Fair Utah," the crowd dispersed amid the music of the combined bands.

At 8:30 P.M. they all reassembled for the dance which was kept up until the dawn of the next day.

Mary "Mame" Elizabeth Woolley attended the Latter-day Saints College in Salt Lake City for one year, was active in plays, gave recitations and became a clerk in Kanab at the "Bowman and Company" general store. She was elected county clerk and later president of the town board, or mayor, of Kanab, Utah, the first woman to be elected mayor of any city in the United States. She married Thomas Chamberlain August 6, 1900, and became the mother of two sons. After her husband's death in 1918, she supported herself and her sons by baking and selling bread to Grand Canyon tourists, and selling women's clothing. She eventually moved to Salt Lake City, where she was an officiator in the Salt Lake Temple. She died August 20, 1953, at the age of eighty-three, and is buried in Kanab, Utah, not far from the ranch where she milked cows and the city offices where she served as mayor.

SOURCE:
Mary E. Woolley Chamberlain: Handmaiden of the Lord, An Autobiography. Privately published in 1981.

Mary Hulet (Coburn)

Born: February 9, 1882, Snowflake, Arizona
Parents: Sylvester Silas and Mary Elizabeth Dalley Hulet

The home where I first saw the light was one log room covered with hand-hewn shingles with a dirt floor. The cracks between the rough logs were chinked and daubed with mud. Half of the room was a bedroom. The other half was a kitchen and dining room.

My oldest brother was accidentally killed when he was five and I was three. Mother has told me how, in true big brother fashion, he always defended me and said, "She is too little to whip." When he died, I lost something very precious out of my life. My one and only memory of Vettie, as we called him, is when he lay in his coffin in our little home.

The next three children were girls, Emma, Kate and Lenora, to my

My father was a good provider and at one time was providing for thirty children. There was only once that I remember we were ever barefooted up until Christmas time and it was not long after that father went to Salt Lake City [from their home in Arizona] and bought a box full of shoes. He would always buy everything wholesale and go to the manufacturers and get the best prices. He would get all sizes [of shoes] and this particular time he had this huge box full. I remember how we all scrambled to get the size that would fit us.

—*Fannie Ellsworth (Greenwell)*

When I was 13, Mother went to Provo for a month or six weeks and left me to do the cooking for Father and my two brothers. Everyday I cried because the boys mussed up the house and scared me with dead mice.

—*Stella Smith Colton (Hardy)*

father's great disappointment. The youngest girl was born while Father was on a mission to England. She was named Lenora May and the way it came about was a standing joke in the family for many years. Father made a very good friend in England whose first name was Lenora and so he wrote: "name the new baby Lenora" and without any punctuation went on to say "May God bless you." He was very much surprised when Mother wrote that she had named the baby Lenora May, but we all liked the name for our blue-eyed baby girl. Father & Mother and all of the children up to that time had brown eyes.

Father was gone three years and [when he returned] the baby was old enough to say, when Mother asked whom she liked "I like my papa, but I don't like that man over there," pointing to Father.

From the time I was old enough I was a baby-tender. I was a very nervous child when I was left with the baby while Mother did the outside chores. Father was often away taking care of his sheep. Mother often returned and found me in a corner with my back to the wall with the baby in my arms, frightened almost to death at imaginary sounds or shadows.

While Father was on his mission to England, Mother taught school. I attended school before I was six but I had already learned to read very well. I was put in a class with boys and girls four or five years older than myself. I always loved to read. I went to play with one of my friends and found a book or magazine I hadn't read, and it was good-bye play. I advanced as rapidly as I could in our little one-room school. I was a precocious child.

I was the teacher's "pet" because I was so much younger and smaller than the others in my class. I prided myself on having good lessons but one day I had failed to learn my

spelling lesson so I went to sleep so soundly it was impossible to awaken me until the spelling lesson was over.

We [often] visited my Uncle Laban Morrill and his wife Aunt Emma, Mother's older sister, at Circleville. They had a little store and it was a delightful privilege to go into the store and help ourselves to lumps of brown sugar and have Uncle Laban give us a handful of jelly beans at a time. Never before had we enjoyed such luxury. One time Katie who was about three went to sleep on the brown sugar sack after stuffing her little tummy to repletion.

When I was about a year old, I took the measles. I caught cold and the rash went in and came out on one leg. It formed a running sore and Mother was unable to heal it. We had no doctors. The nearest thing to a Doctor in our town was Sister Paulina Lyman, wife of Apostle Amasa Lyman. We called her "Aunt Pauliny." Finally Father went to Parowan and got Aunt Pauliny. She told Mother to sew strips of fat bacon on a cloth and wrap it around the infected

When I attended school it was understood with the Principal (George Cluff) that I would stay out of school one day each week to help mother wash, and every morning I had to get up and clean up all the bedrooms before I left for school. Mother liked that day I stayed out, because I would tell her all the gossip about the boys and girls at school. We always did the ironing at night, and about 11:00 P.M. we would stop ironing and eat us a "quiet bite," as mother used to call it. It would consist of eggnog and toast, or cornmeal gruel and toast, but how I enjoyed it.

—*Rebecca Hughes Claridge (Porter)*

On the opposite side of the street from where we were living in Provo was the "Provo Canal" or stream, 8 or 10 feet wide and 1 1/2 feet deep. Almost every day we boys would see fish in this stream, some of them over a foot long. We would wade in to try to catch them, often being able to grab one only to have it get away. The result was wet clothes. I was many times whipped or otherwise punished for this but without any good result.

One day mother stepped to the door to call me. I was in the canal "fishing" in water almost to my waist. I ran home and mother, in a very pleasant voice, said "go to the wagon and take off your clothes." I thought, "Is she going to switch me on my bare skin?"

She followed me to the wagon carrying in her hand a dress belonging to my sister, Theresa. After I was undressed she handed it to me, ordered me to put it on, saying "In your wading you need not get this wet for you can pull it up high enough to keep it out of the water."

Although soon some of my playmates called for me, I would not answer and did not leave my sleeping place until mother brought back to me my own clothes and allowed me to discard the dress and put my own clothes on.

—*William Shipley Burton*

part, changing when necessary. Mother did so and it wasn't long until the leg was well. The neighbors had been telling Mother I would either lose my leg or be a cripple. There is a deep scar on my leg but it is just as strong as the other one.

A few years later there was an epidemic of measles in town. Aunt Thrine, one of Grandpa D's wives, had seven children down with measles and no one to help her. I was about the only child in town who was immune to measles. I wasn't very old but she asked me to come and help her. I could run errands, carry drinks of water to the invalids, etc. I felt very important. Aunt Thrine gave me cloth to make Emma & me a dress. It was white with a red figure in it.

When I was ten or eleven we bought a home in another part of town [in Summit, Iron County, Utah]. Here we had two rooms and a small orchard. One of the apple trees was the joy of our hearts. It was a large tree with spreading branches and in the early fall it would be loaded with sweet little yellow apples. We loved to sit in the comfortable old tree and read a good book. We kept lots of bees and during the honey season I would get fixed up with bee vest and gloves and carry the honey comb slats to the extracting room where the extractor would take out the honey. It was exciting carrying the slats past the swarms of angry bees.

Then we moved to another part of town. I made a bosom pal of Molly Farrow our next door neighbor. Her brother John was my first beau. We used to walk home from the children's parties arm in arm without saying a word until we reached my door when we would say a hurried good night and he would go home and I would go in the house. My first romance.

My cousins Will and Frank Dalley, who lived across the street when we were growing up were a pair of handsome lads and they danced like a dream. They took [the] place of the big brothers I didn't have and often took me places if I had no date. They were dear boys. I loved them. They both died when very young.

In 1896 we decided to move to the Teton Valley. We had two covered wagons all fitted out and ready to go about June 1st, 1896. It was quite a lark for us children. Mother drove one team and father the other.

Sometimes we camped out and made our beds on the ground. After riding all day we were glad to run around and play games. One night while we were playing, a train came tooting down the track, and the smaller children thought it was coming after us and we were frightened to death.

We soon bought a farm and settled down. We had a hard time getting our farming done. We didn't have any hay the first year or two and the cows almost starved to death in the winter. There was no sale for milk and

butter. We children always referred to those days as the Dark Ages.

We made whole families of rag dolls miniature size and made houses for them. We spent

The first tailored coats brought to town were worn by two Clarkston girls Hulda and Josephine Malmberg. They were working in Corinne. They came home one Sunday and walked into church with their new coats. They surely looked mannish, but trim and neat. Mother called them "brazen hussies," but it wasn't long until all the women folk were wearing them.

One incident in my school life, while reading my lesson, I idly put a pin in my ear, as I had them pierced for earrings. On glancing around there was one of my schoolmates who had put a pin through his ear, thinking he would not be outdone by a girl.

—*Catherine Heggie (Griffiths)*

One incident I remember distinctly and with envy: a pair of wedding trousers. A young man had occasion to go to Salt Lake City and while there purchased two seamless bags (heavy cotton sacks used to hold the heavier grain). These he had made into trousers . . . with the red stripes on the sacks on the outside, which made a real lively effect. These trousers were made especially for his wedding costume and were really something new and classy.

—*Livy Olsen*

many happy hours dressing them and playing with them. One day my brother, Marion, thought he would have some fun and he got the butcher knife and began to behead the dolls and accidentally cut the end off his own thumb. Mother immediately clapped it on and bound it up and soaked it in consecrated oil and it grew on.

I remember one Christmas, probably the poorest one I ever spent. Mother had managed in some way to make us three older girls a Christmas dress and we went to a Christmas party at the Church house. We were given a few pieces of candy each. Emma and I saved every piece of ours to take home to the four little boys. We scolded Kate all the way home because she ate part of hers. That was all the little boys got for Christmas. Leonard said "I hope Santa Claus won't always be this poor."

The next Christmas Lenora and I worked for Aunt Lue and Aunt Sophia. Uncle Rob promised to pay [us] when he sold his calves. One of his animals came into our field and while it was there a cattle buyer came and we sold the animal. We took our pay out of it and sent the remainder to Uncle Rob. He is very good natured so I don't think he minded much. Lenora and I decided to have a good Christmas that year so we got out the Sears Roebuck catalog and ordered a nice present for everyone, also decorations for a Christmas tree. When Christmas came we had a tree and all the trimmings and a present for everyone. So we were all happy. Things began to be a little better.

I always loved the gospel and was active in Church duties and activities. My Aunt Annie Dalley, a wonder woman, was President of the

Primary. When I was between 12 & 13 she chose me to be her secretary. With her help I succeeded very well. During this period Sister Zina D. H. Young & Emmeline B. Wells visited our little Primary and I had the great privilege of hearing Sister Young speak in tongues and Sister Wells gave the interpretation. I remember hearing Sister Wells repeat this little poem: "It is a sin to steal a pin much more to steal a larger thing."

I took part in public a great deal such as Primary, Sunday School, Conferences, etc. I gave readings and sang. Esther, one of my playmates, was a natural alto. She and I sang together until we were grown up and I moved away. I remember one song in particular we sang in Primary Conference called "Cuckoo." Esther led out on the Chorus the second time and when she started the third time I stopped and said, "Say, we have sung that Chorus three times already." "We have not," said Esther. To save a hot word battle Aunt Annie stepped up quickly and calmed us down and we went on and finished our song.

[Mary attended high school in Rexburg, Idaho, for three years, and later graduated from the Fremont Stake Academy. She became a certified teacher and taught in several communities.]

I taught the winter term at Driggs [Idaho] for the munificent sum of $35.00 per month. With my consent, at the end of almost every month Mother would come down after my check on payday to buy feed for the stock. I was glad to let her have it. It made me very proud to be able to help the family out. I taught for 25 years.

[While teaching] I couldn't afford a

In October [1852], Father came home and told Mother he was called to move South three hundred miles. Mother felt dreadful bad for she had been separated from her people so much and now we were settled so near them. She thought it was cruel she had to go away so far. We started to go where we were called, Cedar City, Iron County. We were three weeks on the road and very cold weather. Our wagons were made into a corral every night and the men stood guard for Indians. Every precaution was taken on account of Indians.

Many more [settlers] were also called. There was a large company that went when we did to strengthen Parowan and Cedar City. We longed for Lehi again. Oh, I was homesick but we were called and had to make the best of it. Father bought a place and we commenced again. But everything was so different.

—Lucy Hannah White (Flake)

A short time before we reached Bluff, Wayne and Monroe came with some fresh horses and a generous supply of provisions. We were very happy to see them because we knew we would soon arrive in Bluff. One thing I can well remember. They brought some large, juicy watermelons. Oh, I can almost taste them yet. Of course, they were not ice-cold, but they were sweet and juicy and indeed a treat after our long, hard journey. I'll never forget those cheerful campfires we had and the stories and songs we enjoyed by the light of those fires. [When] we laid in bed we could hear the howl of coyotes. They had a mournful sound and sometimes you might think they were suffering, but that was just their way of expressing themselves. I was never afraid as long as Mother and Father were near.

—*Susan Elizabeth Redd (Butler)*

watch so I had to borrow Father's big silver watch of the turnip variety. It was a stem wind and the stem was loose. One evening on my way home I looked down at my watch and to my dismay saw the little stem was lost. It was in the spring and the unpaved streets were covered by water-filled hoof marks and wagon ruts. I felt it was foolish to look for it. So I went back in the school house and knelt down and asked God to help me find it. I got up from my knees and walked out into the street and the first hoof mark I looked into there was the watch stem down in the bottom.

I taught at Lincoln the next three years. I boarded with the Coburns and met the man whom I afterward married, [Frederick Adrian Coburn]. We were married December 19, [1906]. He went on a mission to the Central states on January 26, [1907]. I taught school all the time he was gone and paid his expenses. When he returned we bought a small farm near Weston, [Idaho].

Mary became the mother of seven children. She was among the first to graduate from the Fremont Stake Academy—later called Ricks College—in Rexburg, Idaho. She taught elementary school for several years, worked at a variety of retail jobs, and was very active in fulfilling her church callings. She especially loved genealogy. She died March 20, 1958, in Toppenish, Washington, and is buried in Weston, Idaho.

SOURCE:
Journal. Typescript. Utah State University Special Collections.

Mary Jane Perkins (Wilson)

Born: November 6, 1870, Cedar City, Utah
Parents: Benjamin and Mary Ann Williams Perkins

*Mary Jane, pictured above with her brothers and sisters,
is in the middle of the top row.*

When I was nine years old a call came from Pres. Brigham Young to go and settle . . . in San Juan County, [Utah]. My parents were among the company leaving late in October, 1879. About fifty men and women and ninety children began this long trek across the plains and deserts. The winter proved to be a very severe one and with nothing but wagons and the blue canopy of heaven to shelter them from the cold. Well do I remember the parting when we left our friends and relatives and in fact all we had behind, but like other pioneers—obedience to the call led them in search of their life's mission for such it proved to be. . . .

Well do I recall when we reached the "Hole-in-the-Rock" on the Colorado

My parents had gone to attend a fast day meeting, which was then held on Thursday. My brother and I were down at the Weber River and the thought came to me how we could catch some fish. We went home and I got some needles and linen thread that my parents fetched from England. I took two or three of the needles and heated them so that I could bend them and make hooks. I then took two lengths of the thread and put it through the eye and bent the eye to hold it fast. We used grasshoppers for bait and my brother and I caught eight or ten fish before we heard daddy whistle for us to come home. He was sure pleased.

—*Lorenzo Hadley*

River. Men's hearts almost failed them when they saw what they thought was an utter impossibility to make a road, as the walls of rock were perpendicular and so high that to reach the bottom they had to tie ropes around the men's waists and let them down to the bottom. Again the force that drives men on to duty besieged them and with . . . hearts of determination they began the long task of blasting, and thus began the road down to the river.

My father having a great deal of mining experience in Wales was put in charge of the work and he was christened "the blower and blaster from Wales." It was here at "The Hole-in-the-Rock" that we spent our first Christmas holidays. The children had no place only on the wagon wheels to hang their stockings, never-the-less old St. Nicholas visited them with parched corn and some cookies which were baked in the dutch ovens. However everybody especially the children were happy. And we spent most of the day gathering sage brush to build fires at night to dance by. It of course was not on waxed floors, nor wearing various colored pumps, but it was on the sand rocks and some [children] were bare-footed. Brother Charles E. Walton Sr. being the orchestra. Sometimes he played the violin and other times the cornet. By the sound of this cornet we were all gathered together and knelt in prayer each night before retiring to bed. If the family was too numerous to all get in the wagon, beds were made under the wagon as tents were too heavy to haul.

After six weeks the road was completed. With the aid of chains and ropes and all the men holding to them at the back, taking one at a time, finally all of the women and children were taken down as this was their first experience [crossing the river by ferry]. . . . However all were crossed dry and in safety, with the exception of one boy that was pushed off by some old angry cow but he was soon helped back on the boat.

After many more weeks of travel and hardships the company arrived in [what they named] Bluff, on the 6th day of April 1880. They were not very inviting to look at however, as

I had a vine from which I picked enough grapes one year to buy me a pair of shoes from Judge McCoulough who marketed the grapes in Pioche, Nevada, then a thriving mining camp.

Later, when Robert Lund and Erastus W. Snow managed the store, we had regular stick candy with red stripes running around it. I had all that was good for me as a price for catching mice in the store with the old fashioned mouse trap.

—*Edward Hunter Snow*

The first job I ever had was picking up sweet potatoes for Frank Tyler. I received 25 cents a day for it. I remember it lasted about a week. Boy, I thought I had a lot of money. The next job was driving the derrick horse for Ike Robinson. This was a much better job. It paid 50 cents per day. I would earn five or six dollars at every cutting of hay. Ike asked me one day what I was going to do with my money and I told him I was buying ducks at 50 cents a piece. As I remember, I bought about 15 of these beautiful ducks which I would watch for hours, swimming up and down the waste-way of the millrace. I thought I was really in the money! The next thing I bought was some calves. I had a nice little herd of 15. I kept them around the farm and sold them to Marion Lee for a very nice profit.

—*Edward Maddocks Claridge*

everybody was worn out and glad to get to the end of the long, hard journey, it being sixth months since we left our comfortable homes in civilization and beginning new homes in a wild and desolate wilderness.

They spent their lives trying to conquer the San Juan River and the Indians. Consequently, the long hard trip was only the beginning of what they endured after reaching Bluff.

Mary Jane Perkins married Heber James Wilson on September 17, 1888. They became the parents of twelve children. She served as president of various ward auxiliary organizations and sang in the ward choir for forty years. She was a member of the Monticello city council and served as postmistress for that community. Mary Jane died March 7, 1956, at the age of eighty-five, and is buried in Monticello, Utah.

SOURCE:
Autobiography. Typescript. Utah State Historical Society.

PART FOUR

The Blossoming of Zion

oung persons living in the Utah Territory in the latter part of the nineteenth century witnessed many important changes.

Educational opportunities for young people improved greatly. Teachers received better training, the quality and numbers of schools improved, and study materials became more widely available.

In the Church, the Primary Organization was established for children in 1878. The Young Men's and Young Ladies' Mutual Improvement Associations (YMMIA and YLMIA) became more widely organized. More young men were sent as missionaries to the far corners of the earth to proclaim the gospel and gather the Saints to Zion.

Among the most significant commercial, political, and spiritual events were the completion of the transcontinental railroad at Promontory Summit in 1869, the achievement of statehood for Utah in 1896, and the dedication of Latter-day Saint temples in St. George, Logan, Manti, and Salt Lake City.

Through all these changes, children grew steadily into manhood and womanhood. Decades of hard work, cooperation, fun, and faithfulness prepared the future leaders of Zion and laid the foundation for the spectacular growth of the Church in the twentieth century.

James William Nielsen

Born: August 20, 1887, Fairview, Utah
Parents: Niels Joseph and Minnie Schiller Nielsen

here was a piece of ground on Father's side of the homestead that was ideal clay for brick, so we all decided to go in together and build a kiln of brick. Father did the book work and kept account of all the time each put in, and Uncle George [Davis—actually James's brother-in-law] was in charge of the brick kiln, its building, and burning. Father and George did the molding of the adobes; the rest of us helped mix the mud for the adobes, turn them, and wheel them to the kiln.

We all worked our spare time during the summer, and in the fall the job was completed. The wood for burning was hauled and stacked around the brick kiln until Uncle George said we had enough. We used cedar wood, and the surrounding hills were full of cedar.

The first school I ever attended was the one that Mrs. Gibbs taught in her home on 28th Street just below Washington Avenue. It was a one room house made of logs. She had all of us children in this one room and we only had one book, so while one child was reading from the book, the rest of us were taught to peel potatoes, cut the tops off radishes or some other such work.

—*Mary Elizabeth James (Jones)*

There were seventy-five thousand adobes in that kiln of bricks, our whole summer's work. How happy we all were when the fires were started in the arches and the job was nearing completion.

As well as I can remember, it takes three weeks to burn a kiln of bricks. They must be kept at a certain heat and watched continually night and day. How Uncle George stood the ordeal, I don't know; he was the one that watched night and day. If he ever slept it was only a cat-nap. He watched that brick kiln like a cat watches a mouse.

We took turns helping him, cutting the wood and firing the arches. Then the rains came. It rained night and day for a week, and we finally ran out of wood. We had burned every stick of

wood we [could] find on the place—corrals, fence posts, an outhouse—everything.

We couldn't get off the place for a load of wood as the whole country would mire a saddle blanket. I shall never forget the discouraged look on Uncle George's face when he put in the last stick of wood, looked at the color of the arches, and said, "It will be nothing but a pile of smoked mud."

Father was not a brick maker, but he insisted we seal up the arches as though the kiln was completed and that we all go home to get some sleep.

The next morning, George and I were sitting by the brick kiln moaning the blues, when we missed father and went looking for him. We found him on the east side of the kiln with hands above his head, blessing the kiln of bricks. He was just talking to the Lord and telling Him how we had all worked and did everything we possibly could, and he sealed that kiln into the hands of the Lord.

George and I quietly withdrew; father never saw us, but the effect it had on us, and has again when I write this story, I shall never forget.

When the time was up to open the kiln, most of us were depressed, but father never turned a hair. They opened up the top, and the brick was beautiful, and rang like a bell when clicked together; they were highly colored and sold like hotcakes. They even bought the broken bricks and hauled everything away.

Uncle George said, and most people thought, that the wet weather held the heat in and completed the job, but we children know that it was

My first school teacher was Mary Stocks. She was a very good kind teacher. I advanced quite fast and soon learned to read and write, spell and make figures. When I was ten years old, I was studying reading, writing, arithmetic and geography. English and history were not taught at that time.

I wanted to help earn my own books, so I gathered rags and cleaned them and sent two sacks of them to the Deseret News Office in Salt Lake City. I received a big geography, big double slate, some readers and a hymn book.

—*Alice Ann Langston (Dalton)*

I have a vivid recollection of my first day at Sunday School. I had gone to live in a little town and was a stranger there. One Sunday morning a boy came to my home and asked me if I would go to Sunday School with him. He said: "We have a good teacher."

I did not go with him, but I thought about it. My mother asked me why I did not go. The next Sunday he called again and I went. . . . I sat down near the door so that I could go out unseen if things were not to my liking. After the class work had begun a young man, a teacher with a small group of boys, came down to me and asked my name and invited me to come to his class. . . . He took from the window a copy of Wilson's "Third Reader" and read to us the description of the duel between David and Goliath. He showed us the wood cuts of the shepherd boy with his sling and the great giant with his spear and armor coming forth to mortal combat. It was exciting. It thrilled me! When the class was over, he called me by my first name and said: "We are glad to have you here. Please come next Sunday. That seat right there will be yours." I have been going to Sunday School ever since.

—*Bryant Stringham Hinckley (father of President Gordon B. Hinckley)*

done by the priesthood father held and the power of prayer.

James married Esta Engle on October 24, 1906, and they became the parents of three children. After her death November 22, 1911, he married Janette Davis, and they had nine children. James was good with horses and drove teams on many construction projects in Utah. He worked as a blacksmith, delivered mail pony-express style along the Colorado River, and was the postmaster in Castlegate, Utah. He died March 15, 1976, at the age of eighty-eight, and is buried in Price, Utah.

SOURCE:

"Blessing the Brick Kiln," in *Voices from the Past: Diaries, Journals, and Autobiographies.* Provo, Utah: Brigham Young University, 1980.

Violet Wilson Lunt (Urie)

Born: August 10, 1873, Cedar City, Utah
Parents: Henry and Mary Ann Wilson Lunt

remember Eliza R. Snow [coming] to Cedar City to encourage the production of silk. Many families obtained silkworms and it was the delight of the children to go to someone's home and see the little worms on curtains, in cupboards, and about the house. . . . It was a delight to gather leaves and take them to the homes where the worms were the most numerous. After being invited in with our small offerings of leaves, we would sit and watch the worms at their work. There was no end of fascination in the spinning of cocoons.

. . . Mulberry trees had been planted all over town. It wasn't too long before our sidewalks were covered with purple fruit and children would go to school with purple stained hands, faces and clothing. . . .

[An] event in my religious life which stands as a great day was the day of

In the window of the pioneer store at Wanship, among the bolts of calico and mohair, several beautiful wax dolls were on display and gave pleasure and delight to all the little girls of the town. . . . I said to my mother, "There must be some way I can work and earn enough money to buy this beautiful doll." She was as understanding as most mothers are and said, "My dear little girl, if you will care for the chickens, feed and water them, and gather the eggs every day, you may have two eggs a day to save until you have enough to buy the doll." I was delighted, and you may be sure I didn't neglect my mother's chickens. To add to my can of eggs, I didn't eat the one I should have had for breakfast, so that made me three eggs a day. It would take three dozen eggs before I could buy the doll. . . .

The twelfth day came at last and the last three eggs were gathered. I ran to the tin pan which I kept on the shelf. I reached for it, and to my surprise there were no eggs there. In place of the eggs there was the beautiful wax doll of my dreams. She had the prettiest golden hair and the brightest blue eyes I have ever seen. My mother had bought the doll several days before. The storekeeper had been selling them so fast, mother thought they might all be gone before I could collect all my eggs.

—*Minnie Peterson (Brown)*

my baptism. [From her diary:] "Baptized Aug. 10, 1881 in the old creek. This was a wonderful day in my life. Many of my little playmates gathered and a party was to be given after the baptismal ceremony. Father invited Brother Richard Palmer to assist him so off we went down to the creek. I walked holding the hands of my father and Brother Palmer, my friends marching in the rear. Father baptized me and Brother Palmer confirmed me. Father wrapped a dry shawl around me and carried me home. We had a grand party and I have never forgotten the solemnity and joy of that day."

It was customary for us to be baptized on our birthdays. Winter or summer, the creek was the place of baptism. . . . I heard of at least one case in my youth where the stream wasn't deep enough to baptize an eight-year-old boy. After repeated tries to baptize him . . . the boy broke away from those performing the service and cried as he ran, "I'll be baptized when you can catch me." He was baptized later. . . .

I attended Sister Chaffin's School. . . . We used stone slates and wrote with charcoal. Between uses of the charcoal it was customary for us to wipe the writing or figures off with a rolling motion of the fleshy part of our forearm. It wasn't above us to spit on the slates to clean them a little better and make them really neat looking.

It seems the best time of my life was hearing [immigrant] people speak in their broken English. We would go to Fast meetings and hear the brethren speak in their native tongues, in broken English, and even "in tongues." I look back on those days as being very precious to me.

I knew the Gospel to be true because those fine old people said it was true. . . . With great power they would declare the gospel to be true.

Even [my school teacher] Sister Chaffin added greatly to my religious life. Each morning she would say, "We're going to have a little prayer." She would then say a sweet prayer that seemed as if she were talking to God in our behalf. I loved her for those prayers.

The first newspaper I remember was run by

Bernard Maeser, son of Dr. Karl G. Maeser. He had his newspaper shop in the back of the building where the Parowan Stake Academy was located. A friend and I applied for a job and we got it because we were good spellers. This was my first job at which I earned money and the $3.00 a week pay seemed enormous. How happy I was to get my first pay and run to the Sheep Store and buy a pair of shoes. They cost $3.00—my entire week's pay.

Often I was a shoe breaker in. Sister Jane had some beautiful slippers and I was proud to be asked to break them in. . . . When I was seen wearing them and received compliments, I truthfully said, "I'm breaking them in."

Some people thought that working in a

[The distance from school] was too far to go home at noon so we took our lunch with us. Mother would spread two slices of bread with grease and put between them a slice of fried ham or some bacon. Another two slices were buttered and had jam in between them. She would wrap them in newspaper and tie a string around them. It was so much fun with our friends to sit under a shade tree and eat our lunch at noon. It tasted of the newspaper but was good anyway.

—*Ethel Blain (Larsen)*

On the 4th and 24th of July we were in our young years given ten cents, and felt rich. You'd be surprised to learn how far that dime went. A group of about four of us would go in together. One would buy a dish of ice cream ("homemade" which Joseph Ellsworth made and sold). We'd ask for four spoons, go to a table and all dip in the dish. Another would buy candy or popcorn, etc. And divide it among us. And one always bought a glass of pink lemonade from which we each took a sip until it was all gone. The children's afternoon dance was attended by all on these days, and the boys in all their gallantry would treat us to little candy hearts with printing on them, such as "I love you," "You are cute," "Be Mine," etc. We were flattered, and compared our candies to see who had the nicest sayings.

—*Alice Ann Paxman
(McCune)*

newspaper office was not a suitable job for a girl. Being a typesetter was looked down on by some, but when I washed and scrubbed the ink from my hands, no one could tell what kind of work I did. Everyone else had to do the same—wash and scrub to be clean. I could not see that it made any difference what I did, so [I] loved my work despite talk against it.

Father had built what we called a "turreter" on the top of our house, and in it was housed one of the first bells cast by the local iron works.

It was this bell which called people to church each Sunday and we children had the job of watching the clock and ringing the bell for Sunday School. As we gained enough stature to reach the rope each of us had the privilege of ringing the bell, and it would remain our job until the next one was tall enough to reach the rope.

We had to ring the bell in rhythm. We would say, "One, tum te toe; two, tum te toe; three, tum te toe," up to ten. . . . The bell would ring out loud and clear, and they could hear it all over

town. . . . The bell was also used for funerals and although it was rung the same way it seemed to have a mournful and dreary sound.

Our washings were huge. They usually took 12 hours a day for the kind of washing we did. . . . In town we used clothes lines, but in the mountains we hung our clothes on nearby bushes and it looked as if we were having a real "flag day" with our washing draped over all available shrubbery surrounding our cabin. Sometimes our washings would be so huge that we'd have to resort to fences both in town and out of town.

We even had animals eat our clothes while in the mountains. If we saw one cow in particular going toward the bushes where the clothes were, we would yell, hurry to get sticks, call for help from the men and hurry to get the clothes in even if they were not dry.

We tried to dress according to the city styles, and would be envious of the church leaders' daughters when they came to Cedar City in their high style clothes and their cut bangs and other new feminine styles.

When [hair] bang style came out, we were all anxious to try it. One older lady would preach against it every opportunity she had. She would talk in meeting and put the most gruesome story before us that we would be cursed with scabs and would become bald [if we wore our hair in bangs].

Mother was an actress. She would participate in many plays. I remember one, I believe it was the "Rosematric Veil." Mother was supposed to be stabbed while on stage. After the supposed stabbing she said something, then pressed something against her to squeeze out something red to make

We used to have weekly dances [at school]. The authorities tried to get more of them. The music was furnished by one fiddle maybe and maybe a couple of cans beat together to keep the time up. We had those dances. One problem was we never figured on dancing more than one dance with one girl at a party except maybe the girl we might have taken. We only danced about twice with her. It was all in fun.

—Torrey L. Austin

I met James Henry Porter when I was sixteen, at school. He, with other boys, came from Safford down to the Academy. He asked me at school if I would be to the dance in Allred's Hall that night and I said I thought so, and he said there were some boys coming down from Safford to the dance, so of course I wanted to go so terribly bad. Father said I'd better not go, but mother knew I had a crush on Jim Porter, so she helped me. We had a new carpet to sew up the strips, so mother said at the supper table, "Reby and I are going to sit up tonight and sew up a strip or two of the carpet." . . . So of course Pa went to bed at his usual hour, with mother and I busy sewing on the carpet. When Pa had got into bed, mother told me to hurry and get ready and she would walk over to the dance with me. She told me to be sure and come home at 12:00, which I did, accompanied by my boyfriend Jim. This was the first time I had ever come home with him and from then on, I went with him steady until we were married two years later.

—*Rebecca Hughes Claridge (Porter)*

it appear to be blood. [My sister] Maude, watching the performance for the first time, screamed out: "My mamma's hurt, she's been killed!"

When I was nine I was detailed with Evan Williams who was then ten or eleven years of age, to drive the hogs from the mountain to Cedar City. We drove about 35 pigs from Jones Hollow to Cedar City. We started before daylight. The pigs would get in a bunch and we had to press them hard to keep them moving. We whistled and sang to get them to go along. We would come to a creek and the baby pigs couldn't cross. We would pick them up to help them move and the mother pigs would bare their teeth and come after us. We would throw the little pigs down or over the creek and the mothers would then root and dig and we'd have to start our driving campaign all over again.

At the age of 12 years I was invited by our chorister, Joseph Cosslett, to join the ward choir which was a great honor and one which I have always considered a sacred responsibility. The choir took part in all public functions, both civic and religious, which required constant training. Several evenings each week were devoted to practice.

Our choir sang at funerals, the saddest days of which were during the flu epidemic in 1918–19. We would go to the homes of the bereaved and sing on the porches. I recall one sad occasion when we were singing, the snowflakes came so thickly that we could hardly see. We all had umbrellas over us so that the pages of our books would not become wet, but our tears wet the pages even if the snowflakes didn't.

I first saw [my future husband] John [Urie]

coming through the trees on a beautiful white horse. He appeared as if he were a prince charming riding to rescue a fair maiden—although I was never fair. . . . I was reclining on a low tree trunk . . . and was reading [a book] in the forest.

I heard a noise and looked up from my book, and there was the most exciting man I have ever seen coming toward me on his beautiful horse. This man riding toward me was a complete stranger. He stopped and we talked. Before he left he asked me for a horseback ride date.

John and I rode Dan and Dagen—soft prancers. . . . On one of our rides I fell off, and I cried all night because John had probably seen my petticoats. . . .

John and I were married in the St. George Temple, June 14, 1892. I was 19 and John was 23 years of age.

Violet raised several adopted children and was dearly loved by numerous nieces and nephews, who called her "Aunt Voil." Her husband, a custodian for the local school district, died in 1936, leaving her a widow for the last thirty-one years of her life. She was well known for her beautiful singing voice and sang in various church choirs for more than seventy years. Violet died in Parowan, Utah, on February 7, 1967, at the age of ninety-three.

I was on the ranch most of the next summer [1855]. Sol[omon Hale] and I worked together in the dairy—we did the milking and churning. I have milked as many as from ten to fifteen cows night and morning. We would get our cows close together, and then we would talk love while we milked. We said if we loved each other when we got old enough, like we did then, that we would get married.

. . . We had to do our sparking [dating] on the sly. One method we used was a little ivory book with ivory leaves which could be written on with a pencil and washed off. So one would write the other a note on this ivory book and hide it in a hollow tree. The other would find it and read it and wash it off and write an answer in return and hide it in the same tree.

—Anna Clark (Hale)

SOURCE:
Autobiography. Photocopy of transcript. LDS Church Archives.

Georgina Spencer (Felt)

Born: December 14, 1859, Salt Lake City, Utah
Parents: Daniel and Elizabeth Funnell Spencer

aturday, April the 8th [1876, Salt Lake City, Utah]— . . . We met over at Luella's as a surprise-party to go over to Annie's. Perry accompanied me over there. Annie said she was surprised. I had a very nice time, everybody paid me so much attention. But I made Fred jealous, so he said, because I sat by another person. We had a very nice time coming home. Burt asked if he might accompany me home but I went home with Fred. It was a beautiful moonlight night. I came in and went to bed, but after we was in bed we talked about the party and different boys until we fell asleep.

Thursday, April the 13th—When we got back [from town] we went into the parlor and there we saw Perry and Burt Sherwin. We had a very nice time. Perry told me the wish he wished that I loved him as he did me. I told him I thought I liked him better than he did me but he declared that I did not. They left at nine o'clock. In a little while after, Ben Writer, George A. Richards, and Tom Dawson came they said that they could not stay but a little while as they were looking after Jack. They stayed until ten. I promised to give [Tom] a lock of my hair and he promised if I would give it to him that he would put it in a locket and I told him I would. He brought me home about half past ten. We had a very pleasant talk coming home and when we arrived at the gate we parted with a kiss. When I got in the house I learned from Ma that Fred had been there. He stayed about half an hour and then went home.

Sunday, April the 16th—I dressed myself for Sunday school. We then went to the Funeral. We went up to the graveyard but we did not come home with the carriage. It was a very long walk home. [Tom] went with us. We came home where we found several of the boys. Fred acted so cool to me but I was as bad. I never spoke above two words to him all evening.

Tuesday, April the 18th—Louie came for me to visit the debating society. We went and there we met Fred, Jim, Dan, George, Charlie, Ed, Joe, Terg and John. Fred brought me home and we parted with a kiss.

Wednesday, April the 19th—We had a nice time at the Association. Coming home we had a better time. [Fred] asked me if I had ever thought of the future and he asked me what I thought and I would not tell him. He then asked me if I would give him a lock of my hair. I said I would as I had given one to Tom.

Sunday, April the 23rd—I dressed for Sunday School. I waited for Henry and Johnnie and of course I was late. Tom and I had a splendid time

I never had the opportunity to go to school because the tuition was high and I was the oldest of the family and had to help around the home. We were lucky if we had enough to eat. The youngest children did get to go to school for a while later on. I learned the ABC's from a card I found and when we had our stove I would spell the name of it and also learned to write it.

—*Comfort Elizabeth Godfrey (Flinders)*

On account of having so much work to do, and a lack of money to pay tuition, I had very little opportunity to go to school. When I did go . . . the only books we had were a reader and a speller. We learned nothing of writing, arithmetic, geography and such subjects.

That was all the schooling I had until I was twenty years old, when I went to Spring Valley to work. There I had an opportunity of attending school for three months. It was very embarrassing to begin school with small children, but . . . I was so anxious to get what schooling I could that I studied during recesses and all other times in order to learn as much as possible before school closed.

—*John Staheli*

I started school in the Mount Fort school in Ogden. I remember I had a teacher, Mr. Cowley, who used to hang us up on coat pegs for punishment when we were not on good behavior. I was quite smart in school and was up with the bigger boys in reading, writing, spelling and arithmetic. I went to school about three months a year.

—*James Heber Holland*

talking. He told me that he loved me and had done so for a long time, but I could hardly believe him and he also told me that he was going away. I felt very sorry to hear of that news. We then went up to the Ice Cream Parlor and had some Ice Cream. When we got in we saw Fred and Bessie of which we had an idea of seeing. Fred acted awful sulky. He would not look at me all the time we was there. But I guess he will get over it. We came home and we parted at the gate with a kiss and I never enjoyed anything as I did that walk and talk. He promised me that he would come down tomorrow night if I would be home and I promised him I would—with much love for Tom.

Wednesday, April the 26th—About eight Fred called for me to go to the Association. I saw that he did not feel the same towards me and at the gate he handed me a note saying this: "Dear Georgie, As I don't expect to see you alone so I will write what I would like to say. Do you prefer T.D. to myself or do you like me the best? Please answer tomorrow and oblige. Yours, etc. Fred." I could answer this but I don't know what to do. If I do answer it according to my own feelings I would say I like Fred the best. But that is not saying that I do not like Tom because I hardly know. I have been with Fred the longest. I like both the boys very well. I will just say that I will endeavor to answer that note tomorrow.

Sunday, April the 30th—I dressed myself for Sunday School. We had a very good school. Charlie walked home with me. It seemed like old times to have Charlie walking with me. I think he is a very nice boy. He invited me to come up in the afternoon to play croquet. Fred called for me to go and we went about half past one. We had a splendid time playing. Charlie and I beat them every time but one.

Sunday, May the 7th—I got ready for Sunday School. I got there in time but we did not stay. We took a walk and met Perry. We came back and took another walk and met Burt. We left him and strayed down into the ninth ward trying to find out where Fred lived but we did not find it. We then came home and ate our dinner. After dinner I took a nap and did not awake until Louie came for me to take a walk. I went to meeting. After meeting I met Fred. We took a walk. He told me what Tom said in his letter to Dave. Tom asked Dave if Fred was going with his girl yet and told him to give me his love, but Dave did not tell me. I would like to send mine back if I could. I want to hear from him awful bad. [Fred and I] stood there a while and I never saw anybody look so handsome as he did when he stood leaning on the gatepost looking at me. The moon was shining on him and his eyes sparkled so I think he is beautiful. We stood there quite a while and then we kissed goodnight.

Friday, May the 12th—We went to the party, we had a splendid time. We went in and sat down by George A., Jim Whytock and Dave. George asked me for the first dance. I said I would if Johnie did not ask me and I told him . . . George [had already signed my dance card]. I danced with Johnie the next and Fred the next and Jule the next, Jim Whytock and the next with Jim Snell and the next with Brig Golden and I danced with Fred three times and I danced with Isodore Hourish. When the dance closed . . . Jule [had signed my dance card] for the Schottische

We used to play "Button" at school, and buttons were just as precious to us as marbles were later on. We could pitch buttons at a peg, and the one who got closest got the first shake. All the buttons that lit right side up belonged to him, the next closest to the peg had the next shake and so on till they were all gone. Many times I have had my ears boxed for coming home with no buttons on my clothes.

—*James William Nielsen*

Once a crowd of boys met Mr. Crouch, our school teacher. Crouch was feeling their heads and telling them what certain bumps meant. He found a big bump on Joe Dalton's head and went on to tell what it indicated. When he got through, Joe said "Yes, that's where old Brownie kicked me."

—*James J. Adams*

We used to make chewing gum out of milk weeds and sunflowers. I remember having a big wad of this in my mouth one day while in school. The teacher spied me and said "Sam, you swallow that gum you have in your mouth." I grunted and gulped but couldn't swallow it for it was so large. Finally all were laughing at me, even the teacher. Finally, the teacher said "If you can't swallow it put it in your pocket," which I very quickly did.

—*T. Samuel Browning*

and Dave for a waltz quadrille [as well as] Joe Long and Eddie Wooley and Pat Lynch. The dance closed at half past ten. While I was dancing with Brig Golden he told me that Will Armsby had sent me his love in every letter and I sent my love back.

Monday, May the 15th—The club met. I thought it was splendid. I never saw anybody any nicer than Joe Sharp. If I don't look out I will be in love with him. Fred brought us home.

Tuesday, May the 16th—It was about eight when Fred came. He brought a sack of candy. We had a splendid time talking. He left about ten. I went to bed about eleven and I was thinking of Fred. He looked so sweet I just sat and looked at him all evening.

Saturday, May the 20th—. . .We went up town [and] met Jim W. and he walked home with us. We went and sat on Jote's porch and sat there until ten o'clock. He was telling us his history and I can say that it was very interesting. He held my hand all the time. I like him very much.

Sunday, May the 21st—About six Fred came to go to meeting with us. He stayed until half past six and then Jote came in and we all started together. We walked until meeting time. We had a splendid meeting. Fred came home with us and stayed until half past ten. I never thought that I ever loved him so much as I did that night. He looked so lovely. I went to bed but not to sleep as I was thinking of him all the time. I thought I never loved anybody as well as I did him.

Tuesday, May the 23rd—[Georgina and several other young men and women had gathered in her yard under a tree and were visiting:] Fred & I talked about everything. George came up and put his arms around me, he dared me to put on his hat and I did. Then he dared me to kiss him, and I did. Fred then said that he would not stand it and they settled it in this way, seeing which could throw the other down first. George threw Fred down first. While they were fighting, Charlie and I were talking and they declared that he had his arm around me, which was not so. Fred was awful mad, he would hardly speak to me. The boys then sang, their songs were splendid. They then went away and still we sat there, I did not want to go when I did. It was about eleven when I came in. Fred said that he thought I was the sweetest girl and he loved me dearly. I told him I did not believe him and at last he convinced me. I went to bed right away and was thinking that I just loved him. I also was thinking of George Felt.

Thursday, May the 25th—[another day of Georgina and several other young men and women under a tree:] I sat down by Joe Sharp. I am still in love with him. He was so sweet I have to love him. We had a splendid talk. He said he wrote about me in his journal and I told him I did in mine. He said that he was going to visit the Association next time just to hear me sing. I then bid them good night and came in and wrote in this journal, with much love for Joe.

*Friday, May the 26th—*We came over to ask Ma if I could stay all night with Louie. Ma said I could if I would come home at five o'clock [A.M.].

Soon after I became established with "my crowd" in Nephi, a few of us girls were just leaving our home when three boys passed, [my future husband] was one of them. I asked who he was. The answer was, "George McCune." I thought he was cute and as handsome a boy as I had ever seen, and said so to the girls. The boys crossed the street going north and George gave what we called then a flirtation with his handkerchief, throwing it over his right shoulder which meant, "I love you." The girls said, "That's for you, Alice," and it took root with me.

I didn't see George again until November when a surprise party was given for the twin sisters of our crowd, Cap and Lell Goldsbrough. I met him there! During the evening, I lost in a certain game, and had to "pay a forfeit." I had to stand before the group and say: "Here I stand all ragged and dirty; if someone don't kiss me, I'll run like a turkey."

A moments hesitation, then George came forward and gave me the kiss. At the end of the party, he asked to see me home. I was thrilled. He was then fifteen, I was thirteen years old. From then on whenever he was in town, he was my "beau," and I was his "girl."

—*Alice Ann Paxman (McCune)*

We never had desks in the schools when I was a boy. They were long slab benches and I remember how hard it was for a boy or several boys to sit very long and still on those benches. I remember that I liked to chase the girls with toads. I would usually go a little early [to school] and chase every girl with a toad. Finally, they told the teacher on me and told me she was going to punish me. Well, the day went on, it was just about time to go home. I felt very good, because the teacher had not said anything to me. I thought to myself, well she has forgotten about it. But just a few minutes before the bell rang, the teacher said to me, "Sam, I would like for you to remain after the others all go." I thought, well I am going to be punished. But instead she just talked to me about scaring the girls with the toads and asked me if I thought it was nice. She said, "Do you know that you might scare those girls into hysterics?" Well, I said no, I didn't think of it in that way. Well, a talking like that did me more good than all the whippings she could have given me. I never once did anything like that again.

—*T. Samuel Browning*

We went over again and Fred stayed until after ten. We then went to bed. With much love for Tom, Fred and Joe.

Saturday, May the 27th—[Louie and I] went into the drugstore and Howe Young treated us. I came home and I never was so lonesome. I called for Jote and we took a walk. I came in and went to bed early thinking of Tom up in Brigham [City].

Friday, June the 2nd—I came home and finished some sewing and about half past seven George Felt and Jim Miller came. We sat out in the front yard in the moonlight. It was a lovely night. I never enjoyed an evening better in all my life if I was as deeply in love with George as I was I would of thought I was in paradise. That is not saying I am not in love with him now. They went at a quarter past ten.

Friday, June the 9th—I am thinking of Tom all the time. I want to see him so bad.

Sunday, June the 11th—I went to meeting and [afterwards] came home and took a walk as I was passing our house I saw George and Charlie and they said they had come down to see me and while we were in the front yard Alice, Lizzie, and Annie came along and asked me if I could not go home with them and we consented and Charlie had one arm and G[eorge] the other. I had a splendid time. I am deeply in love with both of them. Charlie gave me a rose and I gave him one. I was as happy as I could be and C[harlie] said he was the same. I think I did pretty good to keep two boys all the evening and Henry had three girls to walk home with him. I am going to press the rosebud Charlie gave to me. He said if I asked to see the one I gave him in ten years from that night I could. There is no use of me trying to hide my love for C[harlie] as I can't do it. On our way back we met Fred. He was just going home. I spoke to him but he did not answer me as he was mad, but I guess he will get over it.

Monday, June 19th—I took a walk with Perry. He was just as lovesick as ever. He hugged me and talked so loving it made me sick.

Thursday, June 22nd—I was thinking if Tom would come down to go on the excursion on the 4th. I hoped he would. I will [be] so glad if he does. I don't know which I like the best. I think it is Tom.

Tuesday, June the 27th—I wished Tom would come down on the 4th. I inquired of the boys and they said that he was coming. Ida Young & Bessie came and sat down when Martha and Ianthus Richards came. We sat there some time and I then asked the boys if they would not accompany us up to Ida's as I was going up to sleep all night. I acted awful mean to Fred. I had a splendid time.

Monday, August 14th—[Maud] came over and we took a walk. She and I walked until it was time to go to the rehearsal. In a short time, we commenced our acting. I did like it especially in the last scene when Charlie and I had to embrace each other. He does act as if he like[s] me. The

Mrs. Stewart [our teacher] was a widow, and she had the entire care of three young children. She used to bring her children, her mending, and her ironing to school, and at recess and noon she would mend or iron. She often allowed the older girls to iron during school hours. This they loved to do. The flatirons were heated on the large, oval stove which stood in the middle of the room.

We used slates entirely for writing, with a slate pencil attached . . . by a string tied through a hole in the . . . frame. Most of the older children had double slates which, of course, furnished more space. The girls usually had a little bottle of soapsuds and a wet rag or sponge for erasing or cleaning their slates. The boys, however, were not so particular. It was quite a task to keep slates clean and sweet smelling since saliva was often used when water was not handy or available.

—*Amy Brown (Lyman)*

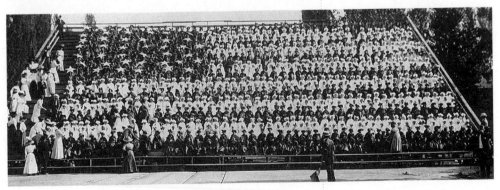

One day a little girl, whose family was a recent arrival, came to our house and said, "Sister Burton, Mother would like very much to borrow your candle molds if you would please let her have them."

Mother handed the candle molds to the little girl. In about 10 minutes the same little girl came again. "Sister Burton, Mother wants to know if you have a ball of candle wick that you will loan her. She hasn't any." The ball of candle wick was handed over.

In about 10 minutes the same girl was back. "Sister Burton, Mother has no tallow. Could you please loan her some?" The tallow was produced and delivered. In a few minutes the same child appeared at the door.

"Sister Burton, Mother does not know how to make candles, could you please come over and show her?" Mother went.

—*William Shipley Burton*

only thing that marred my happiness was Fred. I did not speak to him all evening. I am very sorry that it has happened but it was not my fault. Charlie took me over to Louie's after it was all over as I was going to sleep with her. I bid him good-bye at the gate but before that he kissed me. It was so sweet. He promised me that he would come down tomorrow night. I went to bed immediately. Thinking of Charlie and wondering if he did like me.

This finds me at the end of my first journal but I hope it will not be the last for I find it such a comfort at time[s]. Everything is here. My thoughts and activities, but for anybody else to read them would think they were foolish ones. I think I have had a great deal of trouble with love affairs just for a little girl like myself. I hope I will never have so much in my future as I have in the past, but I guess I will go through it as I have done. In the future I will try and do better about such things.

Georgina married Charles Brigham Felt (the "Charlie" mentioned in her journal) on June 4, 1884. They became the parents of nine children, five girls and four boys. They lived in Salt Lake City, where her husband was an accountant-bookkeeper for the Salisbury Company (a large corporation), and for Salt Lake City. He was also a banker. Georgie continued to sew throughout her life and frequently sat at her treadle sewing machine and created clothing for her granddaughters' dolls. She died May 25, 1947, in Salt Lake City.

SOURCE:
Journal. Typescript. In possession of Martie Fellows Fowles, South Jordan, Utah.

Jacob Watson

Born: December 7, 1877, Farmington, Utah
Parents: William Henderson and Mary Newbold Watson

At the time I was a boy, the boys were dressed in dresses until they were ready to be put in britches—britched, they called it. Dad was . . . born in England, but in a Scottish coal-mining district. . . . His Scottish brogue and some of the Scottish habits were still with him. He wore his kilts. . . .

When I was old enough to be britched—a couple of years old—instead of me getting britches I got kilts. I don't remember anything about them but my mother used to laugh about the kilts. My father just had to have me dressed in them.

My father was both a section foreman and the Farmington station agent on the Utah Central Railroad. We got on the train anytime we wanted and it was only sixteen miles from Farmington to Salt Lake City. Dad often went to

I was almost eight years old when my youngest brother, Fred, was born. That eventful morning being hurried off to school, I suspected that something was going to happen and I told my little friend Ada Burk what I thought. When I went home for lunch sure enough I found my Mother in bed with a little baby in her arms. I was perfectly delighted and wanted everyone to know. My brother, George, who was five years old, did not share my happiness. He threw himself on the floor and said, "I don't want that little red rooster that's dressed up in bed with my Ma."

—Minerva Edmeresa
    Richards (Knowlton)

Salt Lake City for conferences, to go shopping and for other things; and he always liked to have me go with him. . . . I knew the engineer just about as well as I knew my father.

Whenever we got on with the engineer he'd take me and sit me right on his lap; and when it was time to pull the whistle why he'd just tell me how to pull it. When we were pulling into the station he'd give me the bell rope and let me ring the bell. I got a real "kick" out of it. I wouldn't be more than . . . six years old.

I peddled peaches right on the trains when I was eight years old and up to ten. The peaches were some that were a little too ripe to be on the market. They'd bring them to the station and I'd sell them for half. I just had a basket with a strap over my shoulder with a couple of dozen or so luscious peaches and I'd sell them four for a nickel. . . .

One season I earned enough to buy my own clothes and some dress material for my mother. One night, at dusk, I received pay for peaches that I thought was five cents; when I arrived home I found it was a five dollar gold piece.

[My parents] lived right in the station house. It wasn't 20 feet from where my mother's bed was, to the railroad. You could almost step out of her bed and step right on the train. Of course there was a platform between the station house and the tracks and a door that opened out onto the platform. Mother couldn't stand the nerve-wracking of the kids running and the trains passing. She worried about them all the time. Finally she told father, "You've either got to take me to Cache Valley—up to the farm—or take me to Provo to the insane asylum. I can't take anymore of the kids being around these trains."

[The family then moved to Smithfield, Utah.]

During the winter the [Smithfield creek bed] . . . would spread out and freeze into ice. We had a good skating pond there. . . . There was a bunch of boys [who] all had ice skates and we were skating on this pond [near the church square] in the evening. There was seven boys and I was the youngest one, and there were some that were five years older than me. I was about 14 at the time.

One of the boys looked up and saw a light in the old log meeting house. He asked us, "What's going on in the meeting house tonight?" None of us knew anything about it. "Well, let's go over and see." So the bunch of us went over there just a "high-tailing" like little "kids" would. We went rushing in that meeting there—didn't know what it was—with our skates on.

Well, a meeting was on and it proved to be our bishop, Bishop Farrell, having an Aaronic Priesthood meeting. There wasn't a one of our group that was a deacon. Right now the bishop took us "under his wing" and he ordained the whole bunch of us deacons right there that night. . . .

It was [after I was ordained] a Priest that I started going with . . . Sarah Rigby Roskelley. The young men were meeting in one room of the old school house—there were three rooms in that

At Promontory Point, in Utah, I worked for Jesse Knight. He had a wood contract with the Central Pacific to supply wood for their engines. It was cut in three foot lengths. At about ten o'clock I could see the trains coming from the west. There were several on each track. I rushed down there. Someone pointed out Leland Stanford to me and told me that he was going to drive the spike of Gold. There was a silver rail about three feet long connecting the other rails together. There were two spikes made of gold. After the ceremonies were over, a railroad man came around giving all the men free passes back to their homes. They wanted to get them out of the country. They were the toughest men I ever saw. Always fighting and killing each other.

—*Orson Twelves*

I had thirteen offers of marriage and more beaux than that. . . . One man wanted me [for his wife] because I had a good father. . . . Another man wanted me because I looked like his dead sweetheart. . . . [But] because I would NOT say yes to him, although he had lived an exemplary life and paid full tithing thus far, he apostatized and left Utah, going back to his old home in Denmark. I felt deeply for him . . . [but] I could not marry a man I not only could not LOVE, but whose breath was worse than garlic.

—*Minerva Edmeresa Richards (Knowlton)*

school house—and the young ladies were meeting in the other. The men wouldn't go to Improvement meetings [YMMIA] unless they were let out of meeting before the young ladies came out from their meetings [YWMIA]. You can see why, can't you?

The night I started going with [Sarah], there was three Roskelley sisters and about four or five other girls in a row with their arms locked. Well, the boys just started crowding in, breaking them up, and each one was picking out a girl. I just went over to Sarah—she was on the end of the row—and I run my arm through hers and she looked at me and smiled and that was the beginning.

I didn't hook onto her thinking anything more than the other boys did—you know, just boys liking girls. We never broke up but we came so close to it four or five times. Our courting days was more hardship than pleasure because of Grandpa Roskelley's personality. . . . He had an individual personality. He was

140

determined that we would not get married. In fact he felt that I was unworthy of his daughter. He made the [comment] to his girls that there wasn't a man living good enough to marry any of his daughters. . . . For that reason, he didn't love any of the boys that were trying to court his [daughters].

At the time we were married Sarah had eight brothers and sisters, the two youngest was a pair of twins. We would have been married right about the time the twins were born, but it would have taken Sarah away [from home]. And how Sarah's mother did cry when she got those two babies and thought that Sarah was leaving. She didn't know how she was going to be able to scrub [clothes] on the board for all that family. So we decided we wouldn't get married then, but we'd go on seeing each other. The twins were born in July of 1895 and we were married in June of 1897. That's two years you see.

Jacob married Sarah Rigby Roskelley in the Logan Temple, and they became the parents of seven children. He worked as a milk receiver at the Richmond Creamery and later was a chemist for the Morning Milk company in Wellsville. He loved serving in the Logan Temple as an ordinance worker and a sealer. Jacob died August 22, 1968, in Logan, Utah.

SOURCE:
Oral interviews with Jacob Watson in 1968 by Gaylen and Elaine Ashcroft. Published in *Jake, M'Boy, A Biography of Jacob Watson.* Logan, Utah, 1969. Published by the children of Jacob Watson.

One of our neighbors had ducks and we loved to watch them swimming. Once we tried to help a new batch swim and succeeded in drowning them— turned out they were chickens. I recall how upset the neighbor lady was and how she complained to mother.
—*Sarah Sylvia Stones (Herrick)*

There was no recreational center in Richmond, [Utah] and so we did all our playing in the hills east of my home. We robbed bird nests and played follow the leader. We played a game called "Bear." You touched one person and then he'd be bear until he could touch another. We played in the barns in the winter time. We liked to play circus. We got up in the hay and performed acts. If we ever got a new boy to come and play, we'd play jokes on him like "hide the egg." We would use him to hide the egg on—right on the top of his head under his hat. Then someone would try to find it and feel all around. Then they would hit him on top of the head right hard and that would break the egg. It would run down his face and down his shirt.
—*Rulon Francis Thompson*

Maude Turman (Mobley)

Born: August 25, 1891, Mesa, Arizona
Parents: James Rouse and Sarah Catherine Ricks Turman

Maude, shown above with her family, is seated on the right in the front row.

I was well taken care of by older sisters, and Mother always had Indian women in to help. My earliest memories are seeing a group of Indian women on the floor and Mother showing them how to cut out mother hubbards [loose, shapeless dresses], then she taught them how to sew them on our sewing machine. One Indian woman stands out in my memory—"Old Mary." She was a grand old woman and we children all loved her. I was sitting in the high chair eating an apple and got the core in my throat. Old Mary immediately ran her finger in my throat and removed the core. I remember and have been told many instances when the quick thinking of these supposedly ignorant people helped the settlers.

My Mother was generous, and always shared with everyone. Her pickled grapes, which she put up in barrels, also hundreds of quarts of fruit, peaches, pears, plums and of course grapes. We had our own bees for honey and it was a big thrill when the Extractor Man came once a year to take the honey from the comb. I can still taste the honey comb, and of course, honey candy was very popular. We had almond trees, [and] raised lots of sweet potatoes, as they were a treat.

As children, we attended school, had good teachers and always Sunday School, as my Dad was one of the earliest Superintendents of Sunday school. We played all the usual games, but my hobby was climbing trees, and no tree was too big or too tall for me not to climb to the top. If I couldn't be found as a child, they would always find me in a tall tree. I must say I usually spent as much time as I could at the blacksmith shop, watching the sparks fly as Dad pounded the wagon rims and the horse shoes. Of course, I picked up some pretty expressive talk, as these rugged men were very expressive in their language. Dad would send me home and again I would be back there, keeping out of sight. Never will I forget the day when Dad gave me a dime not to tell Mother he was smoking a cigarette. Many is the time I had my mouth washed out with soap, black pepper, and anything else Mother thought would break me of swearing. I hardly knew [the meaning of] the words, but I used them just the same.

We had good food as my Mother and sisters were good cooks. Had our own chickens and cow so there was plenty of eggs and milk. My Mother made wonderful mince meat and, I'll have to admit, that I'd sneak to the place where she kept it and eat it by the hands full.

The trees in our yard were wonderful,

The first school I attended was in a Mr. Robin's home [in Farmington, Utah]. Aunt Hulda Kimball, one of Heber C. Kimball's wives, was the teacher. She was a funny old dear, and if we did anything we weren't supposed to, she'd whip us, and then sit down and cry about it.

I was pretty good at drawing, and liked to draw pictures, but if they caught you drawing a picture on your slate, you were punished. I remember one Valentines [Day], when I was about ten years old, I got the bright idea of painting some pictures on some paper and writing some mushy verses under them, and then selling them to the other kids for valentines. It was a good idea while it lasted and I was doing a land office business when the teacher caught me. I guess he didn't think much of the idea, and he made me stand on a bench where everyone in the school could see me, and made me read those verses. I was crying so hard that I could hardly read them, and the kids were getting a big kick out of seeing me punished. I was terribly humiliated, and for days I avoided all of my playmates because whenever they got a chance they would start reciting some of those verses, like "Roses are red, violets are blue, etc."

—*Laura Smith (Hadfield)*

One night I went with Julia [Sanderson] to visit the Tidwells in upper town. Daws Tidwell and his sister Hanna were playing "Croconole" with Julia and I. We were having a jolly time when all at once Julia gave a gasp and fainted. I got real excited as she looked like she was dead. I did not know what was the matter until Hanna yelled, "Daws, cut her corset strings and she'll be all right!" Daws got his pocket knife out, Hanna unbuttoned her waist and Daws applied the sharp blade. The corset string snapped like a whip lash and unlaced from top to bottom. Julia gave a sigh of relief and came right out of her faint. She had been laced so tight she could not breathe.

—*James William Nielsen*

pepper, fig, umbrella, mostly shade trees. In the summer we slept out in the yard, under the trees, as it was very hot in the house. One big umbrella tree was our favorite, as our Grandpa Ricks [Thomas E. Ricks] came to visit us from Idaho, and he slept under the tree. Shortly after, during a wind storm, it split and we were all heart broken as it was Grandpa's tree. Well, our Dad took an enormous bolt and bolted the tree together and saved it.

Dad sold our place [in 1898] as it was becoming drier all the time and things looked bad in Mesa. We settled in Salem, Idaho, a little farming community about 3 1/2 miles out of Rexburg. Our Dad was not a farmer, but he made a try at it. He planted potatoes and we were all helping harvest them when it started to snow. We had never seen snow so we all raced to the house to tell Mother. It was such a thrill. Dad was just as childish as we were and could hardly wait to hitch the horses to the bobsled and take us for a ride. There was really not enough snow for sledding, and the poor horse had a hard pull.

The Sugar Company was building a big mill close to our place, so Dad went to work there. It was called Sugar City and my Mother and Dad operated a boarding house for the workers.

Maude married Eugene Fitzgerald Mobley on September 29, 1925, in Santa Ana, California. She was musically talented and sang at many church and civic functions. An athletic girl, she played girls' basketball for Ricks Academy, rode horseback to teach school, and loved to swim far out in the Pacific Ocean. Maude died in Los Angeles, California, on September 3, 1964, at the age of seventy-three.

SOURCE:
Maude Turman Mobley, Reminiscence. Typescript. In possession of her daughter, Sarah Ann Skanchy, Logan, Utah.

Our first lighting was from the fireplace. Sometimes we gathered "yaller" brush from Temple Hill and used this to light our reading. Later we used . . . grease on a saucer with a braided rag for a wick. Dad used to read to us by this light. It was so poor he had to sit very close to it and his head would get hot from the flame.
—*Orson Twelves*

I well remember the driving of the Golden Spike. Father took us to see it. I had heard them talking about the iron horse, and when we arrived on the scene of the railroad, I took the whole thing in with steady calmness. I was waiting to see the iron horse and when I finally asked father where it was, he just laughed and told me it was the engine pulling the train.
—*Estelle Dixon (Harper)*

Erma Udall (Sherwood)

Born: September 16, 1882, St. Johns, Arizona
Parents: David King and Eliza Luella Stewart Udall

On April 6, 1893 my father David King Udall, mother, Eliza Luella Stewart Udall, my sister Pearl, age 13, and myself, 11, attended the Dedication of the Salt Lake Temple on its 1st day, Apr. 6, 1893.

The crowd was terrific and from the time we fell into line of the sidewalk of the west wall, down the south walk or wall until we came to the South Gate which took us onto the Temple Grounds which must have taken an hour or so, my feet never touched the sidewalk—I was just carried along with the crowd, packed solid. I can remember women being lifted above the crowd and over our head[s] due to fainting.

I really wanted to start kicking to see if they wouldn't give me space to put my feet to the ground. (Which would have been much worse for me for I might have smothered.)

We had been told by Daddy and Mamma that we must stay very near them or we might get lost. So as we were going through one of the beautiful halls that led up to the spacious Assembly Room where the session was to be held, I cast my eyes around and saw Father and Mother some distance across from me. I quickly made a dash for them and ran into a beautiful wall mirror, and to my surprise I found Father and Mother safely within my reach and was I embarrassed.

We also had been instructed that when Pres. Woodruff began the Dedicatory Prayer that we must close our eyes and keep them closed during the time and not be looking around at other things, but be listening to the beautiful prayer which was being offered. I did as I was told—although as I remember, the prayer lasted 45 minutes.

On opening my eyes as they said Amen I found the room as bright as the morning sun. Every electric light in the ceiling of that beautiful assembly room had been turned on and my thoughts were that the heavens had been opened up to us. It is one of the most beautiful, all inspiring sights I ever expect to see. In those days we didn't have electric lights as now. I remember the shouts they gave of Hosannah! Hosannah! Hosannah! To God and the Lamb, which was given three times in succession. My whole body just tingled and my heart beat rapidly. It was so Heavenly.

. . . It was a time of church-wide rejoicing, this being the 1st temple to be started in the tops of the mountains.

My husband and I were married and sealed

Papa and Mama took me to the dedication of the Salt Lake Temple [April 7, 1893]. I still thrill when I think of what I saw and heard.

I witnessed a "Heavenly Manifestation" at the time of the dedication of the Temple and heard beautiful music, beyond anything I have heard elsewhere. I was only eight years old and saw angels on the ceiling. I have always been grateful for the privilege of attending on that sacred occasion.

—*Alice Minerva Richards (Tate) (Robinson)*

147

Mother did not want us to go swimming in the Weber River. My brother and I used to wonder how she would find it out. She would say, "Well boys, did you go swimming today?" "No, mother, we did not." She would then use a strap on the seat of our pants. We used to wonder how she found out. Finally, my brother said, "I know how she finds out, we look too clean." So the next time we went swimming, my brother said, "we are going to play a trick on mother this time." After our swim in the Weber River, we ran a long ways and got to perspiring rather sufficiently, and then picked up dust and threw into each other's faces. When we returned home, mother asked us if we had been swimming and we told her, we had not. This time she really believed we hadn't.

—T. Samuel Browning

to each other for time and eternity in the Salt Lake Temple on October 9, 1907 and how thankful we have always been for this priceless privilege and blessing we received.

Erma had a deep love for her family and for The Church of Jesus Christ of Latter-day Saints. Her father was the first president of the Arizona Temple. She married William Wellington Sherwood, and they became the parents of five children. Erma was active in her community and the Church, serving in various ward callings, working as state PTA president, and participating in several women's clubs. She died October 23, 1966, in Mesa, Arizona.

SOURCE:
Autobiography. Typescript. In possession of Sue Arnett, Tempe, Arizona.

Francis Washington Kirkham

Born: January 8, 1877, Lehi, Utah

Parents: James and Martha Mercer Kirkham

At my birth I was a very white and delicate child, owing to my Mother sitting up all night with a dead boy (Johnny Mercer) who she loved very dearly, while in a pregnant condition. . . . When I was two days old my father left home to work on the St. George Temple. . . . My father was [later] appointed Tithing Clerk, which position he has since held. How well do I remember walking across the fields . . . with my father's dinner taking it up to town. . . .

On January 22, 1880 my brother Oscar Ammon [Kirkham] was born. A fat plump healthy boy with a voice suitable for a long-eared donkey, yet he had a good heart. . . .

In these times whenever a stranger came to our town we knew it.

Everybody knew one another and everybody was happy, although we did not have so much money then. . . .

We used to buy garden stuff and vegetables then J.M. [my older brother] and I used to peddle them in Salt Lake. Prices were good then and we used to [do] fairly well. When we had poor luck I remember how discouraged we would feel. I would throw myself in the back of the wagon feeling badly. One day a lady set her little dog on me and it broke my heart. I remember tramping the streets all day and then at night going to sleep on one or two quilts on the old Tithing Yard. . . . I used to watch the growth of the majestic Temple in Salt Lake. . . .

In the winter of 1889 and 1890 Ma wanted to send me to school [at the Brigham Young Academy in Provo, Utah] but Pa thought I was too young and so I did not go to school. I had to be the faithful one at the store. Many a book and newspaper have I read while there. Many an hour of my early boyhood have I spent there waiting on customers. . . .

We were all surprised when Pa received a letter from the President of the Church to go on a mission. I was 13 years old. I will never forget my dear mother on that occasion . . . with a smile of peace and satisfaction, proud to be the wife of one so honored. . . . Yet I believe in her secret thoughts she thought of a babe soon to come to . . . her family. God only knows her

Mother had inflammatory rheumatism in her legs and they gave her grief all of her life. I remember times we put oil cloth in the bed and packed snow around mother's legs; and worst of all, I remember her standing in buckets of cow manure that had been heated with warm cow's milk as they considered this a remedy for leg trouble. I don't know if it helped, I only remember that it smelled terrible!
—Sarah Sylvia Stones (Herrick)

thoughts and prayers in the secret hours of her chamber. The servants of God had called my Father and His will was to be done. All things were made ready. Pa was to leave on November 24, 1890. . . .

My mother was taken sick on the Monday previous [to Father's leaving] and gave birth to my little sister Elizabeth Jane, named by my mother on Tuesday. I remember Pa coming to me on the Monday night and asking me to go down to [the home of] midwife Mrs. Lucy Dawson and ask her to come to our house. I was but a child, hardly knowing the meaning of these things. . . .

The child was born and we thought all would be well. I remember carelessly riding our old horse Jumbo down around the old school house. . . . When I returned Pa told me Ma was very sick and not out of danger. How my thoughts have smitten me since for that trifling thing and how I cried unto my God to preserve my Darling Mother. It was on the Friday morning J.M. and I [were] in our little store, we had heavy hearts within our breasts, praying, praying, Oh! how fervently, for [the mother] who had given us life, that now lay unconscious on her bed. Pa had been at her bedside day and night. Kind and loving ones had administered to her. . . . Yes, we had done all. We, the children, had not visited her sick bed . . . as we did not wish to disturb her. It was on that Friday morning, November 21, 1890, that Pa came to us two weeping boys and told us our Mother had left this world of cares. An awful thought, another hurried question to see if it were possible, and I myself gave vent to the tears which had long been choking in my heart.

Mother had lost three children and she was determined to do everything in her power to keep us well. In those days everyone wore the long underwear in the winter. Mother kept a bottle of olive oil on the mantle and whenever we sneezed or complained of not feeling well she would give us a tablespoon of olive oil. I got so I really liked it and didn't mind drinking it. Olive oil was our remedy for most every ailment.

When [my brother] John got the croup . . . I would peel the dry skins from the onions and Mother would slice them then she would put them in a cloth bag, which she had especially for that purpose. The bag was fashioned so it would fit the chest. Then she would pound the onions a bit then put the bag of onions in the oven of the wood stove and warm it until it was nice and warm. Then she would put it on John's chest and pin it to his night clothes. It worked, for John didn't [get] pneumonia.

—*Elizabeth Adelaide Fuller (Dewitt)*

Father made a plow out of a big forked stock and we boys held it in place while our father pulled it. The stick plow was made of quaking aspen. He fastened it to himself by a strap. We plowed two and a half acres that way, and planted wheat. I always remembered that picture of my father doing the work of a horse.

—*George Theobald*

Our [milk cow] had a calf but it died. Father, thinking the cow would do better and be more gentle, skinned the calf, stuffed the hide with straw, and when he milked the cow he would bring out the stuffed calf, lean it up against the fence, drive the cow to it and sit down and milk.

—*James Gale*

Oh! . . . my Mother, kind and suffering, why have you left us in this cold world? But thou art watching over us now. [We who have] struggled and lived, only hoping that thy reward would be God-fearing and virtuous children. . . . Oh God protect her now as she waits for the glorious resurrection. Give her joy and peace in her spiritual home. Protect us, her offspring, that we might live to die as she, virtuous and pure, beloved by all for her deeds of kindness and love. And that we might live lives of Sons of God, worthy of such a noble birth. . . .

We shut the store for the remainder of the week. News spread over the town. Kind and loving hands came to give us assistance. I remember riding Old Jumbo around to tell Aunt Sarah Ann Olmstead to Aunt Abbie Ragal's and few others to tell them the news. Aunt Sarah Ann was on the porch. I called out to her. She asked how Ma was, as the report had gone out that she was a little better. I told her she was dead. She broke into tears of deepest grief. She had lost a sister true and loving. . . . My Mother's death was a surprise to all. . . . What tongue could tell their grief or wonder what a change would come in her demise. . . .

We gathered in our front room on the Saturday. Pa and his children sat on a lounge near the side of the corpse. Pa, when going to see the corpse, first fell senseless on the floor. But he was calm, knowing God knew all for our good. The coffin lid was closed. How well do I remember that face. Peacefully to sleep, that is all. That innocent smile of peace and rest. One last look and she was carried away. Think, ye sons, who know not what this is. One last look on [the mother] who gave us life and we said Adieu until that God who gave us life shall bring us back to Him until the morning of the resurrection of the just. The day was a little cold. I remember being in the back looking on that solemn procession. Sixty-five wagons and vehicles followed [Mother's] earthly remains. A few words at the grave, the thud of falling dirt and all was over. How I loved my dear brothers and sisters. But a week had gone [by] before Father watched the last spark of life of the innocent babe go out and [he] saw the loving spirit of Ma near to carry it away.

This winter Pa was very ill with pneumonia . . . carried down by his burdens. I remember him calling me in once and asking me to give him some holy oil that his cold should cease. As he was getting a little better, he called me in one day to [record] a vision which he had seen of dear mother. He was not asleep but sitting in his chair looking into the other corner of the room. [He] saw mother and babe and other loved ones in a beautiful spiritual world dressed in temple robes. . . . They seemed to keep their hands from Pa to indicate his time had not yet come. . . .

In the winter of 1892 for about 12 weeks I stole myself away and went to school at Salt Lake City where J.M. had been attending. Brother [James E.] Talmage was president when I went, but he soon left and Brother Done was Principal. I [had] just turned 15. . . . Not a soul did I know, but learning and an education—how I craved for

On the corner lot just west of us lived Brother Benjamin Blake and his good wife and family and their home was a real social center for the neighborhood. His five daughters—Caroline, Elizabeth, Emma, Jane and Harriet were hostesses for many evening groups. Bro. Blake could play on the violin and his English wife was a remarkable story teller, so the boys and girls of the neighborhood often dropped in for a little dancing, story-telling, home dramatics, or even a spelling match.

One Sunday evening when a crowd of us were there telling stories, etc., some in the big easy chairs that Bro. Blake had made for his home and some on the sofa, we stayed on and on as young folks will do, little realizing how the time was passing. All at once I roused up from my chair and looked around and every one of us had dropped off to sleep there and the morning sun was coming up in the east. I quietly slipped out the door and went home. I did not need to explain for I had spent so many nights with Jane and Harriet that mother was not concerned at all when she knew I was there.

—*Mary Ann Mansfield (Bentley)*

On my own accord I was baptized March 28, 1893, by Andrew Johnson, in a vat connected with the glue factory of Thomas H. Smart, Sen., which was filled with water heated warm for the occasion.

There seemed to have been quite an era of baptizing at this time [1893], for the Salt Lake Temple was completed and dedicated in April of the same year. It was necessary that we be baptized in order that we might go through it, as did most all members of the Church, to view its interior and attend the dedicatory services.

I was present at the services when the capstone of the [Salt Lake] Temple was laid, and quite distinctly remember seeing President Wilford Woodruff press the electric button which set the stone. I also remember hearing the vast concourse of people present singing the hymn, "The Spirit of God Like a Fire Is Burning."

—*Silas LeRoy Richards*

it. I had a little examination and soon took my studies of business courses. . . . Teachers . . . had noticed my studious ways and had words of praise for me. One little incident shows how sensitive I was. In an examination I had been writing com. law, and knowing the answer, but looked in a book, nervously to see if I was [right]. My teacher saw me [and] told me students had been expelled for that offence. I could hardly keep the tears down but it was a grand lesson for me.

I [returned] home [to Lehi from school]. We had unconsciously sunk into debt a little. The garden was not dug. I remember working all day in the store. . . . Aunt Emma called me Old Faithful. . . . [I was] digging the garden by moonlight.

[In the fall of 1893, at the age of sixteen, Francis enrolled at the Brigham Young Academy in Provo, Utah. At this time he began keeping a regular journal:]

Rules Professor Keeler gave us from the Pen of the best authority.

March 1, 1894

1. Get into a business you like.

2. Devote yourself to it.

3. Be honest in everything.

4. Employ caution, think at a thing well before you enter upon it.

5. Sleep 8 hours every night and more if you need it.

6. Do everything that means keeping in good health.

7. School yourself not to worry. Worry kills. Work does not.

8. Avoid liquors of all kinds.

9. Shun discussion of two points—religion and politics.

10. Last but not least, marry a true woman and have your own home.

Read these over once a week.

May 1, 1894—. . . [In the evening I] went to a Grand May Day Party. I was asked . . . to act as the reception committee. Room D was beautifully decorated and a . . . May Queen party was held. Dancing around the May [Pole] was very nice. It was a draw party, ladies bringing beautifully decorated lunch baskets. I had the very good luck to draw Miss Laura Hickman. She gave me a lovely bouquet of flowers. Dismissed at 12 o'clock.

May 22, 1894—Today is Kindergarten day. Nice program, consisting of singing etc. of little tots of about 4 years old. . . .

February, 1896—Dear old Diary. I have slighted you; but my school days have been so very busy that I have not taken the time to talk to you. My school days are perhaps the happiest days of my life. Since my entrance here at the Brigham Young Academy on the 13 of Jan., I believe, I noticed a young lady, a singer, Miss Sadie Jones.

Well! As luck would have it, I looked at her. She looked at me. Finally, it was Good Morning. At the close of the 5th week, I attended a Leap Year Ball, ladies choosing partners. But I did not go with Miss Jones but went with a Miss Emma Ramsey from Payson (a very nice girl). But the

Mother told me of an experience that has always remained with me. Prior to the death of my sister, Virgil [from diphtheria], my mother awakened one night and her mother appeared in the room leading Virgil by the hand toward the door. Mother said to her, "If you are taking Virgil outside you had better put her bonnet on." Her mother replied, "Where I am taking her, she will not need a bonnet." The next morning, Virgil was feeling so well she was going to get up. She asked for a drink of water; but when mother returned with the drink of water, Virgil had passed away.

—*Rulon Francis Thompson*

155

Mother conceived the idea of teaching school to help make a living. She had only a common education for those days and today it would be considered very common indeed. In those days in the country towns most anything in the shape of a school was appreciated.

Benches were placed on each side of the fireplace and extending out into the room, the third bench was placed across the end forming a square. The pupils were seated facing inside. Mother took a position inside the square and there she ruled supreme.

We had nothing to burn but sage brush which the settlers hauled as part payment on school tuition. One of the boys would be detailed to bring in some brush and replenish the fire, it would blaze up and send out such heat that those nearest the fire had to retreat but not for long, as it would soon die out and they could return to their places. In cold weather this operation had to be repeated about every half hour.

As pay for Mother's services we would receive some flour from one, some potatoes from another, a little piece of meat from another and so on. Meat, butter and cheese were considered luxuries and it was very little we had of that.

—*Ebenezer Crouch*

following Monday Miss Jones showed me an invitation to the Valentine Party in Lehi & she asked me to go over home with her. Of course I did not refuse although I had been home the week previous and heard the Home Dramatic Play, "The Trustee." We left Provo, Miss Jones, myself, Bro. Jones, . . . a cousin & Miss Lillian Metcalf. Our ride across Provo Bench and over muddy roads in an open 2 seated buggy was pleasurable only [because] we were in high spirits.

I drove to May's house and the young ladies were made comfortable. I went home and put on my best duds.

The folks now spring a thorough surprise on me although I had thought to surprise them, Pa says I will soon be called on a mission. . . .

Saturday morning. The girls now wear big sleeves and they powder and paint their faces. . . .

I was called to the telephone about 15 minutes before starting time for the meeting & James M. read a letter from Brother George Reynold's Secretary asking me to be home Sunday Feb. 23 to meet Apostle Teasdale and talk on missionary matters. I will always know how I felt and what I turned and said to Prof. Brimhall & then got up before room D crowded with students, but I got through alright. . . .

Sunday morning Feb. 23, 1896—. . . Went to Sunday School, taught my class subject, the Three Witnesses. Helped pass the sacrament in the Primary. I ate some of Aunt Emma's pudding for dinner & then went to meeting.

Nothing unusual seemed to be there, but presently . . . Apostle George Teasdale came in and soon followed by George Reynolds, President Wilford Woodruff's private secretary. . . .

Brother Francis Salzner, A.E. Bushman, T.F. Trane, Joseph S. Broadbent, Christian Knutson, Frank Butt, Mark Austin, Francis Kirkham, Jos. Russon, Willie Taylor & Hyrum Baker, were present. All but the latter 2 promised to go and the longest time given was to Mark Austin who starts beginning of next winter. The Apostle called each person up by his role asking of his willingness, his native place, etc.

In most instances they were sent to native place. Joe Russon goes to England. He was called about no 8. The Apostle looked at me. Brother Reynolds spoke up & said, "There is Bro. Kirkham's father," pointing to Pa. The Apostle then turned to Pa and asked him if he could send his son to New Zealand. Pa began to answer "I will try" when Bro. Reynolds said "Certainly he can." So I was given my letter and told that I should leave Vancouver Island by April 1, 1896. The Apostle asked my age, I told him I had been 19 one month, he said, "That is a good age to learn a new language" & also said that I had a great work to do there.

My heart was full, as this was the first time that I fully realized that I must go.

I walked home with Pa & Joe Russon. A few tears were shed by our family. Oscar and May both [have] good hearts. . . .

Friday, Feb. 28, 1896—This is my last day at

The first time I ever went for a sleighride with a crowd of young people, Will came to ask me to go riding. Annie answered the rapping at the door. She turned and said, "Will wants you to go sleigh-riding with him." I said, "Oh, can I go?" Father and Mother had gone to a supper at Brother and Sister Yates, and Annie, my oldest sister was left in charge of the house. She said, "Yes, I believe if Mother were here she would let you go." I bundled up and we had a gay time. We passed Brother Yates place several times singing at the top of our voices. Mother remarked to those near her, "There goes a lot of hoodlums," not knowing her own daughter was among them.

—Catherine Heggie
(Griffiths)

The competition between the Mormons and Gentiles was keen. I was at the ball game when Colonel Wade, the Gentiles' crack-shot, was beaten in a shooting contest by a Denarra boy, Cole Roundy. The grandstand was covered with people. [The colonel] shot and everybody cheered. Then the master of ceremonies, Joe Hague, called for the Mormon. Roundy had tied his horse in the brush and walked in. He was dressed in overalls, red bandanna and an old slouch hat. He walked in and raised his gun and without even seeming to aim, shot centering the bull's eye the first time. The Mormons were wild with joy.

—*Lorine Isabel Lamb
(Higbee)*

school at the Brigham Young Academy and this thought never left my mind. . . . In English I resigned from my function as blackboard eraser and also handed in a seniors report. Professor Nelson complimented me on my report and informed the class I was to leave on a mission to New Zealand. My resignation was accepted with a vote of thanks. Many of the students said "good-bye Brother Kirkham & God bless you." Well, good-bye dear old Academy. The happiest days of my life have been spent within your walls. God's choice spirits gather under your roof, and many a prayer and testimony have ascended to our Father on High from your spacious rooms. Oh, never let me forget those companions of my school days, those teachers, whose self sacrificing love has inspired into my heart the Love of God and the love of intelligence. . . . Yes, Good-bye to all you my dearest friends.

Saturday, Feb. 29, 1896—After a farewell to the Christofferson family . . . I went home. . . . The folks all greet me as a departing missionary. Stayed in the store today. At eve, [I attended] the Home Dramatic play "The Rio Grande." Oscar [my younger brother] took the part of an English dude. He did well. Home alone and retired, but let me tell of the song Oscar sang. In his part he sang a song to his girl, Miss Webb. It was so beautiful and sweetly sang that when I thought I would have to leave him for three years I broke into tears.

Tuesday, March 3, 1896—. . . This afternoon Pa, I and Joe Russon [left] on the 4:30 Denver Rio Grande train for Salt Lake City. On our way to the hotel we called into the Assembly Hall and heard Miss Babcock lecture before a Young Ladies Mutual Improvement Association Conference.

Wednesday, March 4, 1896—Today sparks a new epoch in my history. We [went] through the [Salt Lake] Temple. I met there a Maori chief. We went into the Temple at 7:30 A.M. and were [finished] at half past one.

Here, things before obscure were made plain. I consider it the passing point from boyhood to manhood.

Wednesday, March 25, 1896—Arose early. . . . Pa called me in the store. Said good-bye to me with tears in his eyes and said he would not say more. I looked at the store long and carefully, the one I had helped to build and helped to bring it its present worth. . . . Said goodbye to most of the folks at home. At the Depot a very large crowd gathered and I kissed all the girls and

My train trip to Utah with father is among my choicest memories. How he bought me my very first bananas and sticks of candy, how he let me lay my head in his lap and sleep on the train, the many stories he told me, the lines of poetry he taught me and once or twice he and I would sing together and people would leave their seats and gather around us.

One beautiful morning [while we were in Salt Lake City] father took me to the Temple with him. Apostle Owen Woodruff took us through every room, even up to the pinnacle, where we could see the feet of the statue of Moroni. As we were coming down, father said, "Brother Woodruff would you like to hear my little girl sing a Temple song?" So they took me to a large assembly hall in the Temple where I sang a Temple song. Oh, I'll never forget that experience.

—*Julia Eliza Claridge (Ellsworth)*

Tom [Prows] came over to our house one evening and suggested to my sister Lillian that she put a [dough] face on me and send me over to his house to scare some of his family. My sister fixed the dough, rolled it out thin, and I lay on my back while she smoothed it down over my face, then made holes so I could both see and breathe. Then she tied a white cloth around my head in order to hold the dough in place. She then wrapped a white bed sheet around me and started me to the Prows home. We lived 8 or 10 rods north; they had one log room with a willow or brush shed in front. . . . I went through the lot and stood under that shed by a post, facing the door. Josephine, the oldest girl, just my age, opened the door to let a kid go out. She saw me and let out a hideous scream and fell back on the floor. I scattered dough and pieces of that sheet all the way across the plowed ground between our homes.

I was about ready to cry when I made my report to Lillian and Tom as Sister Prows came in. Believe me she was excited and mad. She knew it was some trick of ours. Lillian told her the entire story. She gave us some pretty good council, took Tom, and went home.
—*Edward Lenox Black*

shook hands with men and women. My Sunday School class was there and uncles and aunts.

When the train whistled I kissed May and then Mary Smith and then Sadie said, "Don't forget me." With weeping I did not look around but once. Got on the end of the train and waved my hat . . . until I was out of sight.

Francis Kirkham successfully completed his mission to New Zealand, where he would return twice to fill shorter missions in 1916 and 1962. He married Alzina Robison in 1901, and they became the parents of six children. Alzina died in 1941, and Francis married Marguerite Burnhope in 1942. He was an educator and a well-known scholar of the Book of Mormon. He went swimming at the Deseret Gym in Salt Lake City nearly every day for many years, until just one year before his death in 1972 at the age of ninety-five.

SOURCE:
Journal. Photocopy of holograph. Special Collections and Manuscripts, Harold B. Lee Library, Brigham Young University.

PART FIVE

"Dear Letter Box"
Children's Letters to the Juvenile Instructor

inding things written by young children during the nineteenth century is difficult. Lack of time, encouragement, education, and writing tools meant that most children wrote very little, except perhaps on slates in their pioneer schoolhouses.

Rare exceptions are found in a series of children's letters to the editor in the *Juvenile Instructor,* the first children's magazine in the United States west of the Mississippi River. This biweekly magazine was published by The Church of Jesus Christ of Latter-day Saints beginning in January 1866. Its first editor was Elder George Q. Cannon, a young Apostle.

There were many items of interest to children in the *Juvenile Instructor.* Black-and-white illustrations often featured unusual places and animals, or scenes of adventure. There were songs, poems, gospel-centered stories, and sermonettes. The magazine also included an amazing variety of nonreligious feature articles on topics ranging from the Nile River to dish washing, tiger hunting, ostrich nests, wild turkeys, cathedrals, rules for singers, boomerangs, and animals that hang upside down to sleep.

In 1897, Lula Greene Richards, a talented writer, editor, and poet, started a section in the magazine called "The Little Folks Letter Box." The following notice appeared in the magazine:

"Any little boy or girl, who can write something that the children will like to hear read or sung, may write for the Letter Box.

"Each letter must be short, and have only short, easy words in it, so that the very least child who can read, may read the letters in its box, and the little ones who cannot read, will like to hear them.

"Address Little Folks Letter Box, care of Mrs. Greene Richards, 160 C Street, Salt Lake City, Utah."

Hundreds of children began writing their little letters and sending them to Mrs. Richards. Many of the children mentioned that they had fathers on missions, reminding us that until 1925 the Church called men with young families as missionaries. Many of the children who wrote had lost a father or mother; tuberculosis, smallpox, typhoid fever, pneumonia, and accidents all took a heavy toll in pioneer days.

Some children mentioned the pets they loved—little dogs, cats, lambs, chickens, pigs, calves, rabbits, and even parrots. Finally, many of the children related faith-promoting stories of responses to prayer—help in finding a horse or cow, in protecting a little brother or sister from an accident, in recovering from an illness, or in accomplishing some important goal like learning to play the piano or to quit stuttering.

What follows is a representative selection from the letters of these remarkable young writers. These letters originally appeared from 1897 to 1899 in the *Juvenile Instructor,* volumes 32–34.

About four years ago, a friend of ours went on a mission to Australia and New Zealand, and brought home some beautiful birds: parrots and cockatoos. He gave one of them to us, and we called him Dick.

We tried to teach it to talk, but it would do nothing but scream. We would scream at it, and it would scream back. One day someone screamed at it and it fell down on its back, and the next morning we found it dead. My papa had it stuffed, and now it is in a glass case.

—*Sterling Talmage,*
age 6

DEAR LETTER BOX—Our baby can walk. He could walk last year. He will soon be three years old. His name is Ray. His hair and his eyes are brown.

Last year when the days were warm and dry, the men cleaned out our well. They took the curb away. Baby Ray went out of the house when we did not see him.

Mamma went to look for him. She saw him close by the well. If he took one more step, he might fall down the deep well, and it might kill him. Mamma did not dare to call him, for fear he might start and fall. And she did not dare to run, for fear he would see her and step and fall. So she just walked slowly until she would reach him. Then she took him up quickly, and ran to the house with him. Ray laughed but mamma cried. She kissed baby and then kissed me, and said, "Oh, my lambs. I thank God that His angels take care of you!"

I am
Millie

EDITOR JUVENILE INSTRUCTOR:

Papa had let the cows out in the morning as usual to feed through the day. And they did not come home in the evening as they generally did. So the next morning he sent my brother out in search of them. He started about 8 o'clock and did not come back till about 3 o'clock in the afternoon. He said he had looked every place he thought they could be, but he could not find them.

Mamma asked him if he thought to ask the Lord to help him find them. He said no. So mamma told him to go out again and pray to the Lord to help him find them. He mounted his horse and came back again smiling and seemed very happy because he had found the cows.

Mamma said to him, "You did what I told you to do, didn't you?" He did not answer her, but just smiled and went to take care of his horse. When he came in the house he said that he had prayed to the Lord to help him.

—*Golda Mortensen,*
age 13,
Sanford, Colorado

DEAR LETTER BOX—Something very funny happened in our school the other day. I will tell the children about it.

A very little boy named Ralph goes to school with his sister Lina. When no one was looking at him, Ralph slid off from the seat and rolled under it. He went to sleep there, and no one saw him, or thought of him.

When Lina came from another room, where she had been for one of her lessons, some of the small children had gone home. Not seeing Ralph, she thought he had gone home too.

Everyone left the schoolhouse, and it was locked up.

When Lina reached home, her mother asked for Ralph and they were both frightened. Lina ran to all the neighbors to see if Ralph had gone home with any of the children. Then she went to the teacher, and they both went to the school house and found the little boy, still asleep.

—*Lina Fairlain*

DEAR LETTER BOX—My cousin Alice is eight. I am nine. We both go to school. One day Aunt Julia said to Alice and me, that if we would sew up all the carpet rags for her, she would let us have half the eggs we could find at her place for a month. We sewed as hard as we could when we were out of school. And in a month we had the rags all sewed and had found eggs enough to bring us one dollar and a half. My papa gave us fifty cents, and now we have the JUVENILE INSTRUCTOR for our own paper.

—*Julia Smart*

DEAR CHILDREN—We had a baby named Mary but she died. She was the sweetest baby in the world we thought. When she was only thirteen months old, she knew the pictures of the prophets on the corners of my JUVENILE INSTRUCTOR, and could say their names so we could understand her. And she would sing parts of tunes when she heard them. Mamma and I cried a great deal for her after she died. But one night we both dreamed about her. I thought she handed me my pencil and wanted me to write to the Little Folks' Letter Box. And mamma thought she handed her papa's hymn book and opened it and put her little finger on the first line of the hymn that begins "Peace, troubled soul!" And mamma knew she wanted her to sing. And mamma woke up, kissing her baby and praising God. We knew then that baby Mary was happy, and wanted us to be happy. So we sing a great deal out of the hymn book, which comforts us very much. And I have written this letter because Mary wanted me to.

—*Esther Mooreland,*
age 12,
Salt Lake City, Utah

EDITOR, JUVENILE INSTRUCTOR—I was born at Huntsville, Weber County, Utah, December 23rd, 1881, which was the date that the Prophet Joseph Smith was born. I was baptized the day I became eight years of age. That day I will never forget, as it was a special fast day for all the Saints of God. Soon after I was baptized I was taken very ill with scarlet fever. I was very low and lost my speech for a long time. My parents sent for the Elders and through the anointing of oil and the prayer of faith I was healed. I was ordained a Deacon January 8, 1894, at Huntsville, in which quorum I am still laboring. My father is on a mission to Denmark. He started on the 25th of January, 1896. A short time after he left I hired out to work to help support him on his mission and to help the family. I have earned my own clothes and sent my father $40.00 to help him, so he could buy tracts and do a good work. My desire is to live so I can inherit a place in the Kingdom of our Lord.

—*Henry J. Nielson,*
age 15,
Huntsville, Utah

AN EASTER STORY—Myself and twelve other girls started to the mountains on Saturday, as our parents did not wish us to go on the Sabbath. We started about nine o'clock, with our baskets on our arms filled with bread and butter, cake and eggs. We also had three buckets of milk with us, which we took turns in carrying. The milk was to make ice-cream of, when we should get to the place we had selected for our day's enjoyments.

We were a merry, laughing, chattering crowd, as we trudged along toward the mountain. We arrived at the appointed spot about eleven o'clock. Then one of the girls proposed that we all kneel down and pray. We did so, asking the blessing of the Lord upon us, and that He would protect us during the day. We cooked our "Easter Eggs," and ate our dinner, after which we started up the mountain to where there was snow, which we must reach before we could make our ice-cream. We had not far to climb for there had been a snow-slide, and the snow had slid half way, or more, down the mountain. We had frozen our cream, and started to return to camp, when we heard voices above us. Looking up, we saw two boys just ready to start a large rock rolling down the mountain,

directly toward us; and we heard them shout, "Get out of the way, or you will be killed!" We all ran one way except two, they first started in the opposite direction, then one of them turned and ran towards the crowd, while the other in her fright stood right still. She was exactly in the path of the huge rock, as it came tearing down the mountain with a dreadful sound. It seemed as if the rock must certainly strike her, but just before reaching her, it gave a strange bound, and leaping high in the air, went completely over her head, striking some feet below her. We were all very much frightened, and with hurrying feet we soon reached the camp in safety. We ate our ice cream, and talked over the little adventure we had met with, feeling that our Father in Heaven had heard and answered our prayer, for which we thanked Him. The rest of the day we spent in playing and dancing, until about sunset, when we started for home, which we reached about dusk. We all agreed it was the best Easter we ever spent, and one that will long be remembered by us girls.

—*Jennie Bird, age 12,*
Mapleton, Utah

DEAR LETTER-BOX: Last summer some swallows built their nest under the eaves of our house. And one day there was a big rain storm, and the nest was washed down. After the storm was over, mother and I went out and found the poor little birds under a sack. Two of them were dead, and one was still alive. We felt very sorry for the poor mother bird. My mother nailed a box on the house as far up as she could reach, and put some wool in it to make it warm. Then she put the little bird in the box. Mother Bird soon came and fed it, and was very happy to think her baby birdie was safe. It soon grew big enough to fly away with its mother, and we felt paid for our trouble.

—*Edith Alice Thompson, age 11*

TO THE EDITOR—Nearly every Sunday our teacher asks us to write to the JUVENILE INSTRUCTOR. I am willing enough to write, but am one of that kind that never knows what to say.

I am my mamma's only living boy. Seven months ago my papa died, two weeks ago my seventh sister was born, so you see I can't spend much time writing, but must round up my shoulders to see how good a crop of corn and potatoes I can raise. It's my watering turn today, so please excuse me. I have tried to obey my teacher and hope to improve.

—*Ralph Watson, age 11, Parowan, Utah*

DEAR LITTLE LETTER BOX— My uncle let me have a strip of land, and I have got some watermelons, peas, beans and popcorn planted. They are all up, and I expect to get some to keep for the family.

My mother died when I was only two and a half years old. As I could not remember her, I thought I would like to see her. So I prayed to the Lord that I might see her. And one night while I was down with the mumps, I saw her when I was awake. I saw her real plain. And I have seen her once since in a dream. I think children should pray to the Lord for what they want, and He will hear them.

—*Samuel, age 9, Centerville, Utah*

DEAR LETTER-BOX—My two sisters have been up the creek with a crowd, fishing and berrying; and have come home tired and warm, with plenty of fish and some fruit.

We have any amount of flies here, and they are making quite a meal off me while I write. It keeps me sweating to do two such tiresome things at once, as writing and shooing flies. I think my task is easier than my sisters, though, for they are trying to sleep; and I have an idea the beds will be pretty hard by the time they get up; for they keep pounding them desperately, in their vain efforts to drive off the flies.

—*Mignonette, age 15, "The Ranch," Idaho*

DEAR LITTLE LETTER-BOX—My father died when I was only five years old. Soon after he died my little sister was born. And last January my mother died and left my little sister and me. We have no relatives in Utah. But my sister stays with a family where she is well taken care of. And I stay with another family who are as good to me as my mother. I help do up the housework, can sew, and do many things. I like to read good books, and stories from the JUVENILE INSTRUCTOR. I have been going to school, and read in the Third Reader. Of all the schools, I like my Sunday School best; and love my teachers, they tell us so many good things.

—*From little May, age 10, Newton, Utah*

LITTLE MAY—A feeling of sympathy comes with the reading of your bereaved condition. But there is great joy in the thought that God has promised to be a Father to the orphan. And that He has raised up kind friends to provide for you and your little sister, instead of the dear parents who are gone. God bless you, and the good people who take care of you.

—*Louisa Lula Greene Richards [editor]*

DEAR LETTER-BOX—When I was about five or six years old, my little brother and my niece and I went out to play. Just as we went out, by the street, my Uncle Orson Pratt, who was dead, appeared to me. It frightened me very much, and I took the children and ran into the house. Just after we went in a band of horses came rushing past. I think Uncle came to save us from being killed and trampled upon by the horses.

Your friend,
—*Mary Pratt Gardner, age 11, Richfield, Utah*

DEAR LITTLE LETTER-BOX—I like to go to Sunday School, Primary, and day school. My papa came home from a mission last fall. I am a little lame girl, and wish to ask all the little girls and boys who read this to please pray for me, that I may get well. I have been to the Manti Temple, and hope that I may be able to walk and run with my little playmates.

With love, I am your new friend,
—*Ivy Lowry, age 8, Ferron, Utah*

DEAR LITTLE LETTER-BOX—I have a pet dog; its name is Carlo. It is a good dog. Once I went to my aunt's and it came to find me. When I would go to school it would carry my dinner for me, then when school was out it would come after me and I would give it the dinner basket to carry.

—*Edna Hutchings, age 8, Elsinore, Utah*

DEAR LETTER-BOX—I am seven years old. I have a baby brother and like to tend him, but when he cries I want mamma to take him.

—*Lellie Moselle Halls, Mancos, Colorado*

DEAR LETTER-BOX—The 8th of last February I was ten years old. I will tell you something which happened on that day. A neighbor lady of ours heard something disturbing her chickens. She went to the door and saw it was a lynx, and it jumped at her. She got inside and closed the door, and it jumped up at the window three times. Two of her little boys were playing at a neighbor's and she feared they might come while the lynx was there, and it would hurt them. So she and her little girls, who were with her, prayed that the animal would leave before the boys came; and it went away just before the boys got home. The next morning the lady came over and told us about it. As she went back, she looked in her chicken coop, and there the lynx was. She screamed and papa went over and killed it. It was a very large lynx, measured four feet, and it had killed eleven chickens.

—*Josie Memmott, Scipio, Utah*

DEAR LETTER-BOX—I want to tell you about my pet dog, Clover. When she wants anything she sits up and looks very wise. When we all get ready to go anywhere she sits up right in front of mamma and acts very tickled, as if she were asking to go. She is fond of visitors and babies. She sleeps in the cradle, and when the baby is in the cradle she sits up in front of the rocking chair, as if she were asking if she could have it to sleep in. I think dogs know quite a bit.

—*Donia Holdaway, age 6, Aurora, Utah*

Subscribe and Save!

explore
our state's west coast

ARIZONA HIGHWAYS

GREAT WEEKEND! DESERT SPLASH WITH COLOR EXPERIENCE AN INDIAN POWWOW
Page, Lake Powell Spectacular Spring Wildflowers

☐ **Yes, please start my subscription for a full year of *Arizona Highways* (12 issues) and bill me just $19.** (Outside the U.S., $29.)

MY NAME _____

ADDRESS _____

CITY _____ STATE _____ ZIP _____

COUNTRY _____ PHONE _____

FOR FASTER SERVICE:
Call toll-free nationwide
1-800-543-5432.
In the Phoenix area or outside
the U.S., call 602-712-2000.

SAVE 47% OFF THE COVER PRICE

Visit www.arizonahighways.com to order online. Offer expires 5/31/01.

Treat Friends and Family

☐ **Yes, please start a gift subscription for a full year of *Arizona Highways* (12 issues) and bill me just $19.** (Outside the U.S., $29.)

Gift Subscription To:

NAME _____

ADDRESS _____

CITY _____ STATE _____ ZIP _____

COUNTRY _____ PHONE _____

Gift From:

MY NAME _____

ADDRESS _____

CITY _____ STATE _____ ZIP _____

COUNTRY _____ PHONE _____

SAVE 47% OFF THE COVER PRICE

Offer expires 5/31/01.

Arizona Highways

PO BOX 6018
PHOENIX AZ 85005-9916

POSTAGE WILL BE PAID BY ADDRESSEE

BUSINESS REPLY MAIL
FIRST-CLASS MAIL PERMIT NO. 1095 PHOENIX, AZ

NO POSTAGE
NECESSARY
IF MAILED
IN THE
UNITED STATES

Arizona Highways

PO BOX 6018
PHOENIX AZ 85005-9916

POSTAGE WILL BE PAID BY ADDRESSEE

BUSINESS REPLY MAIL
FIRST-CLASS MAIL PERMIT NO. 1095 PHOENIX, AZ

NO POSTAGE
NECESSARY
IF MAILED
IN THE
UNITED STATES

DEAR LITTLE-BOX—I love to read the little letters and hear what some of the little boys and girls can do. I think little boys can be as useful as little girls if they try. I have three brothers and two sisters, and sometimes I help my little sister wash the dishes and sweep the floor, but I would rather do chores outdoors than to help in the house. We had a Primary fair when I was nine years old and I made a hay rack and took it to it. I love to make little wagons and wood racks but my little brother gets them and then gets them broken.

—*James Orson Allred,*
age 11, Freemont, Utah

DEAR LITTLE LETTER-BOX—I have a little sister three years old. She has a little dove which was given to her over a year ago. Some boys saw it and threw at it, and hit it in the eye. Then they brought it in and gave it to little sister. My little brother likes to see it, but does not like to get close to it because it would peck him. Our cousin wanted to buy the dove, but little sister told him he could have the cat.

—*Jennie Anderson,*
age 10, Monroe, Utah

TO THE LITTLE FOLKS—I will write about the twins we have at our home. On March 27, 1896, mother had a pair of twin boys. They have done well. One is much larger than the other. The little one is the quicker; he walked first. The larger one was so fat he could not hold himself up for a long time. Mother was a twin herself, and my elder brother was a twin, but the other died. When the sheep herds were going to the canyon I bought a sheep, and after awhile she had twin lambs. I was very glad. In a few weeks our old pet cow had a fine pair of twin calves. For awhile it took about all the milk we could get to feed all the twins, babies, lambs and calves. I think I live in quite a twin community.

—*Henry Andres, age 11,*
Spanish Fork, Utah

DEAR LITTLE LETTER-BOX—I live in Lehi, near the sugar factory. My papa has raised beets for the factory ever since it came. Sometimes he gets more money for the beets than at other times. They were not so good last year as they were the year before. The beets have to be thinned out in the spring, and pulled, topped and hauled to the factory in the fall of the year. Last fall we had a good fair in Lehi. I patched a pair of pants and got the prize for having the neatest patch. The prize was a little bureau, with three drawers and a little looking-glass eight inches square. This is my first letter. Next time maybe I will do better.

—*Mary Gray, age 9*

DEAR LETTER-BOX—I will tell you how my ma was healed through prayer. She was sick, and my brother, older than me, and myself went out and prayed for her. When we came in she had begun to get better and she got well. I have four brothers and nine sisters. I have ninety-nine cousins in Monroe.

—*Ida L. Larsen, age 13, Monroe, Utah*

DEAR LETTER-BOX—I like to read your stories. And I like to go to school and Sunday School. I read all the Letter-Box. When I have a piece to speak I can speak it, or a song to sing I can sing it, or do almost anything but turn a somersault.

—*Leroy Coons, age 11, Lyman, Idaho*

DEAR LITTLE LETTER-BOX—I thought I would like to tell your little readers of the sad accident that happened to us. One Sunday we were all in meeting but mamma and my two little brothers, Willie and Lewie, aged six and two and a half years. They asked mamma to let them go to the barn to play. She said yes. In twenty minutes the alarm of fire was heard. Everyone in meeting ran, but nothing could be done; our barn was a mass of flames. Of course mamma knew the little boys were there. After the fire was out, the men worked three hours hunting for them. At last, under the smoldering hay, they found the little charred bodies, one lying across the other.

It seemed more than poor mamma could bear. Papa was not at home; he came that night. Everyone prayed for mamma, that she might not lose her life or her reason. The young girls fasted and prayed for her the next day. An Elder said there was not a child in town that could lisp the name of Jesus but what prayed for us, and the Lord answered their prayers we know. In a little while papa took mamma and me to St. George, and I was baptized in the Temple, and mamma went through and was blessed. She was better after that. In two months the Lord sent us the sweetest little baby girl. We named her Grace. My aunt says it was through the grace of God we have her. Mamma says she was sent as a comfort. I want to be good and comfort poor papa and mamma all I can. I hope my letter is not too long.

—*Theresa Knell, age 8, Pinto, Utah*

DEAR LETTER-BOX—I like the stories in the INSTRUCTOR very much. Five years ago I was sick and lame. My aunt sent me a big dog; his name was Will. He was trained to work like a horse. Father put shafts on my express wagon, and Will would haul my little sister and me two or three miles at a time. In the winter he hauled us on a sled. He took us to school, and would lie still in the corner till recess or noon; then he would romp and eat lunch with all of the school, for everyone liked old Will. He laid down and died on the doorstep a year ago. We children felt very bad.

> —*Brigham Homer,*
> *age 11, Rigby, Idaho*

DEAR LETTER-BOX—I will tell you a story about my pet pig. It is as white as snow. Its mother died when it was born. I bought it for fifteen cents, and raised it on a bottle. It follows me everywhere like a dog.

> —*J. Albert McMurrin,*
> *age 8, Clifton, Idaho*

DEAR LETTER-BOX—We live on a farm and have a few sheep, which I herd a good deal in summer. We also have a dairy about twenty-five miles from the farm, to which a part of the family move every summer, where they milk cows and make cheese. I generally go and help with the moving, then come back and help on the farm—water lucern and catch squirrels. I caught 170 last year, and hope to double the number this summer.

> —*Henry Kunz, age 11,*
> *Bern, Idaho*

DEAR LITTLE LETTER-BOX—I go to school on a horse, and I ride two miles and a half. I am eleven years old, and I have a sister that is five years old in July, and a brother that is fifteen. I like to go to Sunday School. As our letters must be short, I will close.

> —*Louisa Haight,*
> *Farmington, Utah*

DEAR LETTER-BOX—I am the only girl in the family of five children. We have a pet bantam hen; last year she laid about one hundred eggs, after which we set her and she came off with nine little roosters. She was very proud of them and proved to be a very good mother. She would sit on our shoulder and eat corn from our hand. We also have a dog named Pomp. When I play on the organ he will come and sit by me with his head up and howl—we call it singing.
—*Reba Tew, age 11, Mapleton, Utah*

DEAR LETTER-BOX—Last June we had a hail storm here, and a flood came from the mountain and washed our ditch away. The hail was very large and it laid on the ground fifteen days. So we made ice cream for the Fourth of July. This is something that has never been known here before.
—*Silas Edward Earl, age 11, Bunkerville, Nevada*

We have been subscribers to the JUVENILE a good many years before I was born, so my parents say. I used to like to have the Letter Box read to me, but now I enjoy it so much better because I am old enough to read it myself. But I want to tell you about my little dog. His name is Peanuts and he is three years old. He is about as big as a little kitten, and can sit up. We eat candy and chew gum together, and we are very fond of each other.
—*Kitty Bowring, age 8, Salt Lake City, Utah*

Jack has a grand idea : he floats the tub, and Nero tows him.

But the rope breaks, and Nero makes for the shore.

Jack is attacked by a big Swan for trespassing.

With an unfortunate result.

Nero comes to the rescue.

And Jack, having been saved, goes home—sadder and wiser.

DEAR LETTER-BOX—My papa got shot by the bank robbers some years ago and lost his leg; but he is still at work in the shop. He has sent for an artificial leg.

—*Ray Allan,*
Springfield, Utah

DEAR LETTER-BOX—How gladly do I read your contents! I am only a little boy eight years old, but I love to read the JUVENILE for I always find something good in it. My Mamma gave it to me for a Christmas present. I have a pet lamb named Nannie. She follows me all around and will eat sugar and salt from my hand. I love her very much. I went to a little party at the Agricultural College today, given by my cousin. We had luncheon and then played games, after which we had cake and ice cream. In the cake was a ring, ten cents and a straw. The one who got the ten cents would be rich, the one who got the ring would be married first, and the one who got the straw would be an old maid or bachelor. I am sorry to say I got the straw. I think I must close now for I am afraid of tiring you.

—*Earle Robinson,*
Logan, Utah

MY DEAR LETTER-BOX—My father let me go with him to meeting one Friday evening. The men who asked father to go to the meeting showed us things through a glass. The glass made very small things look very large. Some tiny bits of dust looked as large as peas and we could see that they were little sticks and hairs and fuzz stuck together.

A hair off from a man's head looked as large as a skipping rope and instead of being smooth, it was covered with little stems, all pointing downward. I liked the meeting so well, and talked so much about it, that father got me a small glass like the men used, only theirs was large.

My brothers and I found a little heap of small white and brown specks between two irons. Mother told us they were the eggs of some bug.

We took my glass and looked at the specks through it. And we could see that they were like eggs and some of the white ones looked like shells which the baby bugs had crawled out of. They looked about the size of large grains of wheat.

I am finding and saving some things that we like to look at through the glass.

—*Heber G. Richards*

DEAR READERS OF THE LETTER-BOX—The summer I was eight years old, my dear mamma, sister and I went with my grandparents and uncle Simon to the Manti Temple. While there I was baptized and blest by my grandfather Eggertsen, forty-one years from the day on which he was baptized into the Church; so it was a great day for him. I fasted that morning and felt very happy.

I had the chance of going all through the Temple, and mamma took me in one of the small rooms and prayed with me. And that night when I prayed, I felt as though I were talking to God and He was pleased with me. My big brother had gone to heaven, and he was such a good boy. We miss him very much. I want to be like him and help to make mamma happy.

Once President Woodruff took me on his knee, and blest me, and told me to grow up and be a comfort to my mother. And he told me about his dear mother when he was a little boy.

I had the honor of marching with the Sunday Schools in the Jubilee march, and of seeing President Woodruff crowned. I attend Deacon's meeting so as to learn what I shall have to do when I am a deacon, which I hope to become when I am twelve years old.

—*Lehi Eggertsen Cluff,*
age 11,
Provo, Utah

DEAR LETTER-BOX—I have lived in Lehi right by the sugar factory for four years; and I have seen them make sugar lots of times. I wish all of you children could see them make it.

I help churn, and wash dishes for mamma, and help tend my little baby brother. I don't like to wash dishes very much but mamma thinks little boys ought to do house-work as well as girls. I have read the History of the United States, and am reading the Book of Mormon.

—*J. Hamilton Gardner,*
age 9,
Lehi, Utah

DEAR LITTLE LETTER-BOX—In the spring of 1894 I had a severe spell of heart-failure. The doctor gave up all hope of my recovery and said it was almost impossible for me to get well. But my father and mother had great faith in the Lord, and after my grandpa and papa administered to me I slowly recovered. At times my Uncle Charles L. Olsen would come and play some of the sweetest music on his violin. That, too, seemed to give me new life.

Hoping we may all trust in our Heavenly Father, I will close my little letter.

—*Lizzie O. Borgeson,*
age 8,
Santaquin, Utah

DEAR LETTER-BOX—I will tell you of something which I saw last week which almost made me cry.

A family moved to another part of the city, and either forgot to take their cat or intentionally left her behind. The poor animal stayed around the empty house for several days, without having had a bite to eat. I wish the owners could have seen her sitting at the door, crying to get in, and no one there to hear her cries.

She has failed greatly, and unless someone takes her in, she will surely die from starvation. I would have taken her home, only we live so far from the center of the city.

On behalf of poor, dumb animals, I say, "When you are moving, don't forget to take your cat."

The animals' friend,
—*John Porter,*
Salt Lake City, Utah

DEAR LITTLE LETTER-BOX—I would like to encourage the children to try and keep the Word of Wisdom. I have never drank tea and coffee, and have not eaten pork for almost two years and feel blest by so doing.

—Lottie Larsen, age 11,
Monroe, Utah

LIST OF PHOTOGRAPHS AND ILLUSTRATIONS

left, Douglas, Leland (Leet), Felix (Fee), 1916. The boys are wearing Sunday suits borrowed from George T. and Sarah Dunkley Benson family in Whitney, Idaho. One of the suits belonged to the future prophet, Ezra Taft Benson. Photograph from Barbara Edwards.

Page 167. Three boys on bull. Photograph from LDS Church Archives.

Page 168. Second child of Rot Livingston with pup. Photograph from Kaye Watson.

Page 169. Baby photos in beehive shape. Photograph by Charles E. Johnson.

Photograph from Special Collections, Merrill Library, Utah State University.

Page 169. Lucile Anderson and Virgil Thompson, cousins from Richmond, Utah. Photograph from Elaine T. Ashcroft.

Page 171. Erastus "Rass" L. Jones with his wagon and well-trained ewe, in front of the Lehi W. Jones home in Cedar City, Utah. Photograph from York F. Jones.

Page 172. Youth in Cupid costume. Photograph from Special Collections, Merrill Library, Utah State University.

Page 173. Picture story of a boy floating in a barrel. Engraving from the *Juvenile Instructor,* vol. 29, page 719.

Page 174. Frank and Charlie Canfield. Photograph from LaRae Johnson.

Page 175. Lucretia Vern Seely (Winters), daughter of John Henry and Margaret Peel Seely, born in Mt. Pleasant, Utah, in 1895. Photograph from Margaret Winters Madsen.

Page 176. Caroline Hymas, of Hyde Park, Utah. Daughter of Benjamin and Hanna Thurston Hymas. Photograph from Sharon S. Knapp.

LIST OF SOURCES

Adair, Florence Ellen Fowler. Autobiography. In *Our Pioneer Heritage,* 20 vols., compiled by Kate B. Carter, 7:269–71. Salt Lake City: Daughters of Utah Pioneers, 1964.
Born: April 28, 1860
Sheffield, Yorkshire, England
(immigrated to Utah 1863, age 3)

Adams, James J. "Mormon Diaries, Journals and Life Sketches" (COLL MS 18), Special Collections, Utah State University Merrill Library, Logan, Utah.
Born: October 2, 1848
Springfield, Illinois
(immigrated to Utah 1849, infant)

Andrews, William. "Mormon Diaries, Journals and Life Sketches."
Born: September 2, 1854
Philadelphia, Pennsylvania
(immigrated to Utah 1857, age 3)

Austin, Torrey L. Transcript of oral interview by Jessie Embry, Charles Redd Center for Western Studies, Brigham Young University, Provo, Utah.
Born: December 9, 1882
Liberty, Idaho

Banford, Samuel. "Mormon Diaries, Journals and Life Sketches."
Born: September 22, 1845
Worcestershire, England

Baxter, John M. *Life of John M. Baxter.* Autobiography. Salt Lake City: Deseret News Press, 1932.
Born: June 3, 1859
Salt Lake City, Utah

Beatty, John T. "Mormon Diaries, Journals and Life Sketches."
Born: May 25, 1869
Toquerville, Utah

Beck, Margaret Simmons Bennett. Autobiography. In *Heart Throbs of the West,* 12 vols., compiled by Kate B. Carter, 9:385–89. Salt Lake City: Daughters of Utah Pioneers, 1948.
Born: June 23, 1848
London, England
(immigrated to Utah 1857, age 9)

Bentley, Mary Ann Mansfield. "Life Sketch of Mary Ann Mansfield Bentley, 1838-1935," Special Collections and Manuscripts, Harold B. Lee Library, Brigham

Young University, Provo, Utah.
Born: April 11, 1859
Salt Lake City, Utah

Berg, Johanne Marie Thomassen. Autobiography. Typescript in possession of Paul Thomassen Jr., South San Francisco, California.
Born: November 27, 1844
Christiania, Norway
(immigrated to Utah 1860, age 16)

Berry, Lovenia Nicholson Sylvester. Autobiography. In *Our Pioneer Heritage,* 7:399–403.
Born: June 24, 1854
Springville, Utah

Bigler, James T. Transcript of oral interview by his grandson, Roy Bigler Davis, Salt Lake City, Utah.
Born: January 22, 1868
Farmington, Utah

Bishop, Ann E. Melville. Autobiography. In *Heart Throbs of the West,* 9:434–35.
Born: May 20, 1856
Fillmore, Utah

Black, Edward Lenox. Journal. Typescript. Utah

State Historical Society, Salt Lake City, Utah.
Born: June 11, 1868
Rockville, Utah

Brown, Minnie Peterson. Autobiography. In *Heart Throbs of the West,* 9:445–46.
Born: 1865
Fredirtric, Denmark

Browning, T. Samuel. "Mormon Diaries, Journals and Life Sketches."
Born: April 15, 1860
Ogden, Utah

Bryant, James. Autobiography. In *Our Pioneer Heritage,* 6:61–65.
Born: May 31, 1857
Bleyne, Barmarthan, Wales (immigrated to Utah 1862, age 5)

Burton, William Shipley. *A Biographical Sketch and Some Things I Remember.* Typescript in possession of Janet Seegmiller, Cedar City, Utah.
Born: September 27, 1850
Salt Lake City, Utah

Butler, Susan Elizabeth Redd. *The Family of John Topham and Susan Elizabeth Redd Butler,* compiled by Karl D. Butler. Provo, Utah: Brigham Young University, 1990.

Born: December 14, 1880
Harmony, Utah

Cannon, Annie Wells. "Passing Thoughts," *Woman's Exponent,* 15 April and 1 May 1893, page 157.
Born: December 7, 1859
Salt Lake City, Utah

Chamberlain, Mary Elizabeth Woolley. *Mary E. Woolley Chamberlain: Handmaiden of the Lord, An Autobiography.* Privately published, 1981.
Born: January 31, 1870
St. George, Utah

Christensen, Regina Mary Simmons. Autobiography. Typescript. Special Collections, Utah State University Merrill Library, Logan, Utah.
Born: May 14, 1886
Salt Lake City, Utah

Claridge, Edward Maddocks. Autobiography. Typescript. In *The Children of Samuel Claridge,* edited by Helen Ruth Claridge Cole. Salt Lake City: privately printed, 1987.
Born: May 14, 1882
Orderville, Utah

Clark, Mary Louisa Woolley. Autobiography. Typescript. Special Collections and Manuscripts, Harold B. Lee Library, Brigham

Young University, Provo, Utah.
Born: July 6, 1848
near Goosecreek, Nebraska (immigrated to Utah 1848, infant)

Clarke, Annie Elizabeth Frost. "Mormon Diaries, Journals and Life Sketches."
Born: August 13, 1860
St. Louis, Missouri (immigrated to Utah 1861, age 1)

Coombs, Ellis Day. Autobiography. Typescript. Special Collections and Manuscripts, Harold B. Library, Brigham Young University, Provo, Utah.
Born: March 1, 1883
Mt. Pleasant, Utah

Cox, Isaiah. "Mormon Diaries, Journals and Life Sketches."
Born: June 5, 1859
Mt. Pleasant, Utah

Crosby, Hannah Adelia Bunker. Autobiography. Typescript. Utah State Historical Society, Salt Lake City, Utah.
Born: April 25, 1853
Ogden, Utah

Crouch, Ebenezer. Autobiography. Typescript. Special Collections and Manuscripts, Harold B. Lee Library, Brigham

Young University, Provo, Utah.

Born: September 23, 1850
Tumbridge Wells, Kent, England

Dalton, Alice Ann Langston. "Mormon Diaries, Journals and Life Sketches."
Born: February 5, 1865
Rockville, Utah

Davis, Melissa Jane Lambson. Autobiography. In *Our Pioneer Heritage,* 12:107–9.
Born: November 13, 1846
Winter Quarters, Nebraska
(immigrated to Utah 1847, infant)

Dewitt, Elizabeth Adelaide Fuller. Autobiography. Typescript in possession of Kimberlee Ann Dodds Dray, Provo, Utah.
Born: March 26, 1897
Mesa, Arizona

Dimmick, Charlotte Roper Nielson. Transcript of oral interview by her grandson, Darrell George Conder, 1960. In possession of Marjorie Conder, Salt Lake City, Utah.

Edwards, Martha Jane Miles. Journal. Typescript in possession of Billie Edwards Reese, Logan, Utah.
Born: January 10, 1885
Payson, Utah

Ellsworth, Julia Eliza Claridge. Autobiography. Typescript. In *The Children of Samuel Claridge.*
Born: April 8, 1887
Thatcher, Arizona

Felt, Alma Elizabeth Mineer. Autobiography. In *An Enduring Legacy,* 12 vols., 7:193–232. Salt Lake City: Daughters of Utah Pioneers, 1984.
Born: May 1, 1855
Landskrona, Malmohus, Sweden
(immigrated to Utah 1861, age 6)

Flake, Lucy Hannah White. Journal. Typescript. Special Collections and Manuscripts, Harold B. Lee Library, Brigham Young University, Provo, Utah.
Born: August 23, 1842
Knox County, Illinois
(immigrated to Utah 1850, age 8)

Flinders, Comfort Elizabeth Godfrey. "Mormon Diaries, Journals and Life Sketches."
Born: January 13, 1861
Salt Lake City, Utah

Gale, James. Autobiography. In *The Ancestors and Descendants of James Gale,* compiled by Mae Gale

Wilkins McGrath. N.p., c. 1957.
Born: May 6, 1846
Sydney, Australia
(immigrated to Utah 1857, from California)

Garner, Jane Sprunt Warner. "Mormon Diaries, Journals and Life Sketches."
Born: March 4, 1863
Kimarnock, Ayrshire, Scotland
(immigrated to Utah 1864, age 1)

George, Roy. "Mormon Diaries, Journals and Life Sketches."
Born: February 14, 1880
Mendon, Utah

Gledhill, Sarah Sophia Moulding. "Mormon Diaries, Journals and Life Sketches."
Born: March 7, 1858
Philadelphia, Pennsylvania
(immigrated to Utah 1861, age 3)

Goodrich, Lydia Merrell. Autobiography. In *The Goodrich-Merrell Story,* compiled by Ruth Goodrich and Gladys S. Jacobson. Moses Lake, Washington: n.p., 1975.
Born: February 20, 1876
Paradise, Utah

Greenwell, Fannie Ellsworth. "Mormon Diaries, Journals and Life Sketches."

Born: April 29, 1862
Salt Lake City, Utah

Griffiths, Catherine Heggie.
  Autobiography. Special
  Collections, Utah State
  University Merrill Library,
  Logan, Utah.
Born: March 4, 1867
Clarkston, Utah

Hadfield, Laura Smith.
  Autobiography. Typescript.
  Utah State Historical
  Society, Salt Lake City,
  Utah.
Born: May 27, 1858
Juab County, Utah

Hadley, Lorenzo.
  Autobiography. Typescript.
  Utah State Historical
  Society, Salt Lake City,
  Utah.
Born: November 6, 1851
Derbyshire, England
(immigrated to Utah 1863,
  age 11)

Hale, Anna Clark. *Memoirs of
  Anna Clark Hale.* 1965.
  Special Collections and
  Manuscripts, Harold B.
  Lee Library, Brigham
  Young University, Provo,
  Utah.
Born: April 19, 1841
Clark County, Ohio
(immigrated to Utah 1848,
  age 7)

Hall, Julia Hanson. "Mormon
  Diaries, Journals and Life
  Sketches."

Born: January 28, 1860
Glenwood, Iowa
(immigrated to Utah 1861,
  age 1)

Hansen, Caroline Pedersen.
  Autobiography. In *Our
  Pioneer Heritage,*
  12:66–71.
Born: September 3, 1859
Bindslev Sogn, Hjorring,
  Denmark
(immigrated to Utah 1866,
  age 7)

Hardy, Stella Smith Colton.
  Autobiography. Typescript
  in possession of author.
Born: June 6, 1880
Provo, Utah

Harper, Estelle Dixon.
  Autobiography. In *Heart
  Throbs of the West,*
  9:447–49.
Born: August 6, 1861
Napa County, California
(immigrated to Utah 1865,
  age 4)

Harris, Katherine Perkes.
  Autobiography. In *Heart
  Throbs of the West,*
  9:436–37.
Born: May 12, 1861
Bellville, Illinois
(immigrated to Utah 1862,
  age 1)

Harrison, Eva Christine Beck
  Zimmerman.
  Autobiography. In *Our
  Pioneer Heritage,* 8:48–51.
Born: May 12, 1851

Aichelberg, Shorndorf,
  Wurttemberg, Germany
(immigrated to Utah 1864,
  age 13)

Hatch, Sabra Jane Beckstead.
  Autobiography. In *An
  Enduring Legacy,* 5:145–55.
Born: October 20, 1853
Salt Lake City, Utah

Hatch, Sarah Doney. In *Heart
  Throbs of the West,* 9:438.
Born: October 17, 1858
Payson, Utah

Herrick, Sarah Sylvia Stones.
  Autobiography. Typescript
  in possession of Joyce
  Mount, Spokane,
  Washington.
Born: January 8, 1892
Wilson Lane, Utah

Higbee, Lorine Isabel Lamb.
  "Mormon Diaries, Journals
  and Life Sketches."
Born: January 8, 1862
Virgin City (Pocketville),
  Utah

Hill, William Henry.
  Autobiography. Typescript
  in possession of Janet Bair
  Tolman, Bancroft, Idaho.
Born: April 25, 1842
Skillington, Lincolnshire,
  England
(immigrated to Utah 1862,
  age 20)

Hinckley, Bryant Stringham.
  *The Autobiography of
  Bryant Stringham Hinckley,*

edited by Ruth Hinckley Willes. N.p., 1971.
Born: July 9, 1867
Coalville, Utah

Holland, James Heber. Autobiography. Typescript in possession of Deleta Holland Selvage, Hyde Park, Utah.
Born: October 3, 1869
Ogden, Utah

Jones, Mary Elizabeth James. "Mormon Diaries, Journals and Life Sketches."
Born: June 17, 1866
Ogden, Utah

Knowlton, Minerva Edmeresa Richards. Autobiography. Typescript. Utah State Historical Society, Salt Lake City, Utah.
Born: May 11, 1858
Salt Lake City, Utah

Lamb, Elizabeth Zimmerman. Autobiography. Typescript in possession of Gaylen and Elaine Ashcroft, River Heights, Utah.
Born: October 24, 1831
Quincy, Pennsylvania
(immigrated to Utah 1851, age 19)

Lambert, George Cannon. Autobiography. In *Heart Throbs of the West,* 9:269–384.
Born: April 11, 1848
Winter Quarters, Nebraska
(immigrated to Utah 1849, age 1)

Larsen, Ethel Blain. In *Life Under the Horseshoe: A History of Spring City,* written and edited by Kaye C. Watson. Salt Lake City: Publishers Press, 1987.
Born: July 4, 1886
Spring City, Utah

Lindsay, Sarah Ann Murdock. Autobiography. Typescript. Archives Division, Historical Department, The Church of Jesus Christ of Latter-day Saints, Salt Lake City, Utah. Hereafter cited as LDS Church Archives.
Born: March 2, 1853
Salt Lake County, Utah

Lyman, Amy Brown. *In Retrospect—Autobiography of Amy Brown Lyman.* Salt Lake City: Relief Society General Board, 1945.
Born: February 7, 1872
Pleasant Grove, Utah

McCune, Alice Ann Paxman. "Autobiography of Alice Ann Paxman McCune. a.d. September 16, 1870. Written 1957. With biographical Notes Added by George M. McCune in Tribute on Her One Hundredth Birthday, a.d. September 16, 1970," in

McCUNE, n.p., c. 1970, pp. 1–22. LDS Church Archives.
Born: September 16, 1870
American Fork, Utah

Murnane, Lillie Barney. Autobiography. In *Heart Throbs of the West,* 9:439.
Born: January 8, 1862
Springville, Utah

Murphy, Eliza Ann Lamborn. "Mormon Diaries, Journals and Life Sketches."
Born: April 16, 1858
Bath, England
(immigrated to Utah 1864, age 6)

Nielsen, James William. "Blessing of the Kiln: 1912." In *Voices From the Past: Diaries, Journals, and Autobiographies.* Compiled by Campus Education Week Program under the direction of Division of Continuing Education, Brigham Young University, Provo, Utah, 1980.
Born: August 20, 1887
Fairview, Utah

Nixon, Hannah Isabell Fawcett. Autobiography. Typescript. Utah State Historical Society, Salt Lake City, Utah.
Born: January 17, 1845
Nauvoo, Illinois
(immigrated to Utah 1850, age 5)

Olsen, Livy. Autobiography.
Typescript. Utah State
Historical Society, Salt
Lake City, Utah.
Born: December 1, 1856
Copenhagen, Denmark
(immigrated to Utah 1857,
infant)

Perkins, Cornelia Adams.
Autobiography. In *Heart
Throbs of the West,*
9:432–34.
Born: 1886
probably Parowan, Utah

Perkins, Daniel.
Autobiography. Typescript.
Utah State Historical
Society, Salt Lake City,
Utah.
Born: January 9, 1887
Bluff, Utah

Porter, Rebecca Hughes
Claridge. Autobiography.
Typescript. In *The Children
of Samuel Claridge.*
Born: April 21, 1877
Orderville, Utah

Richards, Silas LeRoy.
Autobiography.
Holograph. LDS Church
Archives.
Born: October 25, 1882
Union, Utah

Robinson, Alice Minerva
Richards Tate. Personal
record in private
possession of George F.
Tate, Orem, Utah.

Born: August 10, 1884
Farmington, Utah

Shaw, Annie Hermine
Cardon. "Mormon Diaries,
Journals and Life
Sketches."
Born: January 23, 1861
Marriott, Utah

Skidmore, William Lobark.
Diaries. Holograph. LDS
Church Archives.
Born: September 22, 1844
Philadelphia, Pennsylvania
(immigrated to Utah 1855,
age 11)

Smart, Rachel Elizabeth
Pyne. Autobiography.
Typescript. LDS Church
Archives.
Born: February 4, 1870
Norwich, Norfolk, England

Smith, Joseph Fielding. "The
Salt Lake Temple,"
Improvement Era 56 (April
1953):224.
Born: July 19, 1876
Salt Lake City, Utah

Smith, Orson. "Mormon
Diaries, Journals and Life
Sketches."
Born: July 4, 1853
near Keokuk, Iowa
(immigrated to Utah 1853,
infant)

Snow, Edward Hunter.
"Mormon Diaries, Journals
and Life Sketches."

Born: June 23, 1865
St. George, Utah

Sorensen, Vera Blain Larsen
Downard. *In Life Under the
Horseshoe: A History of
Spring City,* written and
edited by Kaye C. Watson.
Salt Lake City: Publishers
Press, 1987.
Born: October 18, 1893
Spring City, Utah

Sperry, Harrison, Sr.
Autobiography. Typescript.
LDS Church Archives.
Born: March 24, 1832
Meca, Ohio
(immigrated to Utah 1847,
age 15)

Staheli, John. "Mormon
Diaries, Journals and Life
Sketches." Typescript of
autobiography also found
in LDS Church Archives.
Born: May 28, 1857
Amarswile, Turgan,
Switzerland
(immigrated to Utah 1861,
age 4)

Theobald, George. "Mormon
Diaries, Journals and Life
Sketches."
Born: May 22, 1848
Newport, Isle of Wight,
England
(immigrated to Utah 1851,
age 3)

Thompson, Rulon Francis.
Autobiography. Typescript.

Privately printed and distributed by family.
Born: September 11, 1900
Richmond, Utah

Twelves, Orson. "Mormon Diaries, Journals and Life Sketches."
Born: October 22, 1851
Lincolnshire, England
(immigrated to Utah 1856, age 5)

Udall, David King. Autobiography. In *Arizona Pioneer Mormon, David King Udall, His Story and His Family, 1851–1938.* Written in collaboration with his daughter Pearl Udall Nelson. Tucson: Arizona Silhouettes, 1959.
Born: September 7, 1851
St. Louis, Missouri
(immigrated to Utah 1852, infant)

Udall, Ida Hunt. *Mormon Odyssey: The Story of Ida Hunt Udall, Plural Wife,* edited by Maria S. Ellsworth. Urbana: University of Illinois Press, 1992.
Born: March 8, 1858
Hamilton's Fort, Utah

Urie, Violet Lunt. Autobiography. Typescript. LDS Church Archives.
Born: August 10, 1873
Cedar City, Utah

Warner, Mary Ann Chapple. Autobiography. Typescript. Utah State Historical Society, Salt Lake City, Utah.
Born: October 26, 1862
South Moulton, Devonshire, England
(immigrated to Utah 1868, age 5)

Webb, Francis Adelbert. Autobiography. Typescript. LDS Church Archives.
Born: March 20, 1853
Big Cottonwood (Holladay), Utah

West, John Clements. "Mormon Diaries, Journals and Life Sketches."
Born: June 3, 1861
London, England
(immigrated to Utah 1872, age 11)

Young, John Ray. *Memoirs of John R. Young, Utah Pioneer 1847, written by Himself.* Salt Lake City: Deseret News, 1920.
Born: 1837
Kirtland, Ohio
(immigrated to Utah 1847, age 10)

INDEX